Gaza: when the sky rained white fire

Musheir El-Farra is the Chair of the Sheffield Palestine Solidarity Campaign in the UK. He was born in 1961 in Khan Younis, southern Gaza. El-Farra is a political and human rights activist and a public speaker who has worked for justice for the Palestinians all his life.

He frequently contributes articles to Arabic newspapers on social and political issues. He has also written, coordinated and narrated documentary films on Palestine.

El-Farra took part in a Free Gaza Movement protest to break the Israeli naval siege of the Gaza Strip: on 23 August 2008 two fishing vessels were the first to enter Gaza port in 41 years.

Gaza: when the sky rained white fire

Musheir El-Farra

To Dear Mary
in friendship & solidarity
and lots of admiration
for your hard work for
justice for the Palestinians

Musheir

18 17 16 15 14 13 12 7 6 5 4 3 2 1

First published 2012 by Sheffield Palestine Solidarity Campaign,
118 Upperthorpe, Sheffield, S6 3NF

British Library Cataloguing in Publication Data

A catalogue record for this book is available from the British Library

ISBN 978-0-9574083-0-2

Cover Design by David Campbell
Printed and bound in Great Britain by Bell and Bain, Glasgow

Contents

To my gorgeous sons Qasem and Qayis, who never fail to add meaning to my life; to my beloved daughter Dana, who is so precious to me: I dream of a day when they and all Palestinians can witness a Palestine that is free of occupation, disposition and abuse of human rights; a Palestine in which all people live equal regardless of race, sex, religion or colour.

To the memory of the two people who shaped what I am, good and bad, my beloved late parents Qasem and Laila, and to the memory of my beloved late brother Mones, who accompanied me during the preparation of this book, but did not live to see it through.

Acknowledgments

I would like to express my most sincere gratitude to Muhammed Al-Majdalawi, a fine young promising Palestinian, who worked hard in the Gaza Strip arranging the interviews with the families of the victims and fishermen, and providing logistical help. Muhammad is the third generation of 1948 Palestinian refugees fighting for the rights of his people – a clear challenge to all Zionist assumptions that the Palestinian refugees will eventually forget their homeland, pre-1948 Palestine.

Many thanks to the Al Dameer Association for Human Rights in Gaza for providing me with the documentation of many of the cases in this book.

To the National Society for Rehabilitation in Gaza for their help locating victims who suffered disabilities during the Israeli war on Gaza and organizing visits to them.

To Paul Kelemen, Angela Marten, and Richard Pitt for their help. To David Campbell for the art work.

To Haytham Bayasi and Basma Ghalayinin for help with the translation of the Al Dameer documents.

My deepest gratitude to Charlotte Hubback; without her help this book would have never been finished. Above all, my most sincere thanks are for the families of the victims who were so graceful in meeting me and talking about their tragedies.

Foreword: The human face of inhumanity

In August 2011, a regional court in the city of Haifa told Rachel Corrie's parents that their daughter, Rachel, was to be blamed for her death – being crushed by an Israeli bulldozer – since she was in a war zone. Civilians who are in a war zone, according to this Israeli court, have no immunity from being killed or wounded. The people of Gaza live in what official Israel considers almost permanently a war zone and indeed their lives do not seem to count or to bother the Israeli generals and politicians.

I was aware of this Israeli perception of Gaza as a killing field where anyone living in it is a legitimate target for army fire, in the days leading to Operation Cast Lead. The Israeli press, at that time, reported extensively on the way the army prepared for operations in the Gaza Strip. The army attacked dummy Gazan cities and villages as if they were invincible bunkers of the most sophisticated and best armed force in the world – hence aerial bombardment, heavy gun fire from land and sea and elite units were prepared for the destruction of human life that eventually took place on the ground.

In Israeli eyes the Gaza Strip is an enemy bastion that since 2005 is manned by radical and dangerous Islamists and therefore there is even added justification for collateral damage and blind genocidal policies of the people who live there. One hopes that decent and reasonable people around the world see how false and ruthless is such a perception and how destructive and barbaric is its implementation.

But judging by the world's inaction so far in the face of the continued siege in the present and the unwillingness to demand justice for the 2008 massacre, one feels that the struggle for truth and justice for Gaza has to continue relentlessly and constantly.

This book is one crucial and highly significant part of this struggle. In a detailed, sensitive and a very perceptive way, the truth comes out through interviews of survivors of that massacre, as well as from the personal memories of the author, himself from Gaza. Through his and their eyes, we can appreciate what life in Gaza was like, what it could have been and how it is experienced today.

The strip is neither a battlefield nor a training camp for fanatic radicals. It is first and foremost a human space with normal human beings striving to lead normal life in an abnormal reality. The book asks us to consider this struggle through the unimaginable suffering the people whose stories are told in this book, have gone through. From the moment they were hurt to their torturous recovery – that in many cases has still not arrived – their stories are a human testimony to the inhumanity Israel wrought upon the people of Gaza.

The stories are interwoven with personal recollections and jointly they make up a powerful testimony that could and should be heard in a court that never convened and are part of a call of justice that has not as yet be administered. The impulse here is not revenge and the description and analysis are bereft of any hate towards the state and the people that brought this 'fire from the sky' on the Gazans. This is a record for the future, since so many of those who tell the truth are the children of Gaza whose dreams and childhood had been ruined, but maybe not forever – one hopes a different future still awaits them. We record, so that people would not forget the crimes or the criminals. Acknowledging it, especially as it is done here with the acumen and humane style of a son of Gaza, now a refugee in Sheffield, is the first step towards justice which is the door through which peace and reconciliation can enter.

Professor Ilan Pappe

Preface

The idea for this book started with a phone call from the London law firm Bindmans. They asked me if I could help obtain statements from families affected by the Israeli attack on the Gaza Strip at the end of 2008 and the beginning of 2009. The Israeli military had codenamed it Operation Cast Lead. Bindmans were representing a group of Smash EDO campaign activists who, on 17 January 2009, raided EDO MBM Technology, an armaments factory in Moulsecoomb, Brighton. According to Sussex Police, 'extensive damage, estimated at £200,000 [US$304,000], was caused'. The activists claimed that they had performed a 'citizen's decommissioning' of the factory in response to the war on Gaza. The police also arrested several other people outside the factory, on suspicion they, too, were involved.

Since 2004, there had been numerous protests and direct action calling on the EDO corporation to convert its factory to civilian use. The campaign of protest, civil disobedience and non-violent direct action against EDO in Brighton had come to be known as the 'Smash EDO Campaign'. The protesters have always argued that the company is acting unlawfully by supplying weapon systems for the F15 or F16 bombers, unmanned aerial vehicles, Paveway bombs, or Hellfire missiles. These supplies helped to perpetrate war crimes by UK and US forces in Iraq and the Israeli forces in the West Bank and Gaza. As a result, many Iraqis and Palestinians have suffered serious injury or loss of life, the destruction of their property and of essential local facilities such as water, power supplies, schools and markets.

Although the activists admitted to sabotaging the factory, their defence was that criminal damage was legally justified if the damage inflicted was to prevent greater damage to other properties – in this case, homes in Gaza. The 'lawful excuse' defence was invoked, according to which it can be lawful to commit an offence to prevent a more serious crime.

The activists were cleared in July 2010. The jury accepted their defence that they had acted to prevent Israeli war crimes during the 2009 Gaza War.

To help in the preparation for their case I obtained information from the Al Dameer Centre for Human Rights in Gaza on many events that showed solid grounds for bringing Israeli leaders and military personnel to the international court in the Hague on war crime charges. I passed the information to Bindmans.

The case files passed to me by Al Dameer shocked me. I regard myself as a person who is reasonably familiar with what happened in the Gaza Strip during that war but the documentation in these files (though containing the barest of details) was devastating. They included the date of the incident, the numbers killed and injured and brief witness statements from survivors. The initial idea was to translate these into English, to show the international community further evidence of Israel's war crimes in the Gaza Strip. However, to fill in the personal details I decided to meet some of the families of those killed and injured. It was only then that I began to understand what they had been through.

There are already many reports from human rights organizations which have condemned Israel for war crimes committed. The principal aim of this book is different. It is to shed light on the lives of the victims and their families, and to recover something of the dreams that were shattered and the hopes and aspirations that were extinguished. The pain of those who survive has to be a spur to solidarity with the Palestinians' struggle.

The testimonies presented here were obtained under oath, in a society where oaths are taken very seriously. In almost all cases there were several witnesses to each event recounted and the facts were cross-checked. The evidence accumulated from the testimonies is overwhelming: the Israeli military massacred defenceless civilians in Gaza during December 2008 and January 2009.

It is only a fragment of the Palestinian story since they were forcibly driven from their land in 1948, in what was a case of ethnic cleansing by Zionist militias.

What follows is not by any means a full documentation. To do that would take teams of investigators, gathering evidence over a long period. The experiences recounted here provide an insight into what many others also went through and their stories, too, deserve to be told. This book is a call for justice for all the victims and their families.

Introduction

They were ordinary Palestinians, on an ordinary day, sitting inside or sleeping where they thought they were safe. Outside, children were playing football, cycling or chewing sugar cane. Some women were shopping for dinner. Many were elderly, sitting outside their houses as Gazans do. They all thought there was a truce; and then suddenly their lives were shattered by a hail of rockets, missiles, phosphorus bombs and bullets.

On the morning of 27 December 2008 Israel launched Operation Cast Lead. It was Israel's most devastating attack against the Gaza Strip since its occupation of Palestinian lands in 1948. The attacks lasted for 23 days. It resulted in the killing of more than 1,400 Palestinians. Almost a third were women and children caught in Israeli firepower in the streets, in the marketplace and in their homes. Five thousand three hundred Palestinians were injured, many ending up with permanent disabilities. Hundreds of thousands are still suffering psychological trauma. According to a Palestine Monitor factsheet, 3,500 homes were completely destroyed, some 2,800 sustained heavy damage, and some 16,000 were lightly damaged. These had been homes to about 325,000 people. Seven out of 12 electricity lines were shut down; the power station operated only 50 per cent of the time. One million people were without electricity, and half a million people were without running water. More than 1,000 factories, businesses and private sector institutions were damaged.

The weapons deployed against Palestinian civilians were among the most lethal Israel possesses: F15 and F16 jet fighters, Apache helicopters, drones, naval force, tanks and armoured vehicles, rockets and missiles. It also systematically used internationally banned weapons including: white phosphorus; ammunition containing DTME; and flechette tanks shells which spray thousands of darts over hundreds of metres, ripping apart anyone in the killing zone.

Since March 2006 Israel has imposed a siege on the Gaza Strip. The Israeli PR machine managed to persuade sections of international public opinion that the siege was in retaliation for the kidnapping of the Israeli soldier Gilad Shalit. The truth is different. The Gaza Strip was frequently, and on occasions very tightly, closed by the Israeli occupation army from 2000. Durations were deliberately varied from weeks to months, making planning a journey virtually impossible. The siege was an act of collective punishment, illegal in international law. It was aimed at undermining the democratically elected Hamas government. As a result, patients suffering from cancer, kidney failure or serious heart problems, women with pre-natal complications, and babies in need of specialist care were denied treatment. By mid-September 2010, 376 fatalities resulted from Israel preventing Gaza's population accessing medical services.

The indiscriminate nature of the attacks is apparent from the number of cases where houses were destroyed on top of the inhabitants. Om Ahmad Balosha still hugs the photo of her five daughters, closes her eyes and imagines them in their white wedding dresses. 'Instead, the Israeli army,' she said, 'put them in white coffins.' The five Balosha sisters – Tahreer, 17, Ikram, 14, Dina, 8, Jawahir, 4, and Samar, 2 – were killed whilst sleeping, just before midnight, on the second day of the attacks, when the Israeli F16 jet fighters bombed a mosque adjacent to their house in Block 5 of Jabalia refugee camp.

Dr Izzeldin Abuelaish's daughters, Bisan, 20, Mayar, 15 and Aya, 13, along with a niece, Noor, were killed in their own apartment in Jabalia, on the afternoon of January 16, when a pair of Israeli tank shells ripped through their bedroom. Seventeen others sheltering in the same building were injured.

Dr Abuelaish was described by The *New York Times* (17 January 2009) as a Gazan and a doctor who had devoted his life to medicine and reconciliation between Israelis and Palestinians. 'This is how they repay me,' he said. 'Were they armed when they were killed? They were not armed with weapons, but rather, with love; love for others.' Dr Abuelaish is a rarity: a Gazan working among Israelis, one of the few Gazans with a permit to enter Israel because of his specialist skills.

Despite the Israeli siege and oppression of the Palestinians, prior to the attack on Gaza Dr Abuelaish had worked in Israeli hospitals delivering babies and working on research alongside Israeli doctors. Three of his daughters, including his eldest, Bisan, who was killed in the attack, attended a peace camp in New Mexico for Israeli and Palestinian girls, run by an Israeli. The Palestinian mainstream is opposed to such 'peace' initiatives because they imply the conflict is the result of a misunderstanding or lack of communication that can be resolved by getting to know each other. This evades the root of the conflict, which is that Israel is carrying out military occupation, settlement expansion and ethnic cleansing.

Israel claims 'during the operation the enemy has been fighting from within civilian targets'. But Dr Abuelaish, his family, witnesses and local human rights organizations have testified that their house did not harbour any fighters.

Iman Hamdan told me, 'I still do not believe that my three lovely children have died.' Her daughters Haya, 12, Lama, 5, and her son Ismael, 10, were killed by a bomb. 'I remember them every fraction of every moment. How can I forget them? Every time I look out on our garden, I see them playing as they used to do.'

Their father, Talal Hamdan, recalled the last moments of their lives: 'On 30 December, at 7.45 in the morning, they went to put the rubbish in the container near our house as they did every morning. I was woken up by the sound of an explosion. I did not think much of it. We live in Beit Hanoun on the border, we are used to frequent Israeli bombings. My eldest daughter Sabrin rushed into my room screaming hysterically, 'They killed my brother and sisters.' My three children were targeted by an Israeli drone. By the time I arrived at the hospital, my two daughters had already died. Ismael was bleeding from the brain. The following day he, too, passed away. This is a residential area. There were no fighters here.'

Iman is still worried about the psychological state of her other daughter Hanady, 18. 'She goes to school but without getting anything from it. She keeps saying "I want to die. I should have died with my brother and sisters; I want the Israelis to kill me."'

Talal said, 'They were wonderful kids. Haya was very bright; she always read her elder sisters' books. She was a good Dabka dancer, too. Ismael loved nature; he liked planting things in the garden. They were always around me: not anymore. Iman is coping better than me, maybe she is stronger because she experienced the killing of her father by the Israelis in the first Intifada.'

On 6 January 2009, the Israeli army bombed the Al Dayah family while inside their house, a four-storey building in Al Zaytoun, a neighbourhood in Gaza. They killed seventeen members of the family. The youngest was a 4-year-old boy called Kawkab.

The attackers showed no mercy to medical crews trying to help the victims. Arafah Hani Abdul Daiyem, a paramedic, was in Beit Lahia at the north of the Gaza Strip attempting to reach some of the injured when his ambulance was hit by a rocket. It killed him and two of his colleagues. To add to the tragedy, his family's house was bombed while they were receiving condolences for his death. Three of his relatives, including Arafat Abdul Daiyem, a 13-year-old child, were killed. Dozens were injured. There are other accounts similar to Arafah's.

Many civilians were executed by Israeli soldiers in cold blood, as in the case of the Abed Rabu sisters and their grandmother. Their father Khalid Abed Rabu recalled their tragic deaths: 'We were inside our house; suddenly an Israeli tank took up position near our house on the fourth day of the land attack. It was 7 January 2009. The Israeli soldiers ordered us to come out of the house. I came out with my 62-year-old mother, my wife and three of my daughters. We were all waving white pieces of cloth. We walked a few steps; two soldiers ordered us to stop. A few moments later, a third soldier came out of the tank and opened fire from his machine gun at my daughters. I carried the bodies of my daughters and dragged my mother back into the house. My brother phoned immediately for an ambulance.

We heard the noise of an engine approaching, then the sound disappeared. I looked through one of the windows of my house; I saw the soldiers beating up the ambulance crew. The tank then crashed into the ambulance. By then two of my daughters – Amal, 2 years, and Suad, 7 years – had died. My third daughter Samar, who is 4, and my mother continued to bleed. Amal's last words to her mother, while she lay dying on her lap, were "Do you love me, Mum? Can I have some sweets?"

'Two hours passed, during which all attempts to contact the Red Cross and Palestinian ambulances failed. Samar started to request water, innocently asking me, "Baba, should not injured people be taken to hospital by ambulance?" I could not bear this anymore. I carried Samar out. I decided to either lose my life or save my daughter.

'I walked out to the front of the house. The soldiers waved at us to get out of the house. I went back and asked everyone to get out. My wife and I carried the bodies of Suad and Amal while my brother Ibrahim carried my injured daughter Samar. My other brothers put my injured mother on a bed and carried it. We put all our surviving children in the middle so they were flanked by us on either side. We walked towards the hospital while heavy gunfire from Israeli soldiers continued all round us. As we passed the house of one of our neighbours he brought his horse and cart to help us. The soldiers opened fire, injuring him and his horse. We then realized the only way is to continue walking for over a kilometre to reach Jabalia town. When we arrived there the locals rushed to help us. Samar is paralyzed for life as a result of her injury. She has been receiving treatment in Belgium.'

Human Rights Watch has confirmed many Palestinians were killed while waving white flags. Rawhiah Al Najar, a 40-year-old mother, was one of them. After midnight on 12 January 2010, the Israeli army started shelling the village of Ikhza'a, east of Khan Younis. The shelling continued for hours, causing many fires which the locals tried to extinguish. At 5 a.m. the tanks entered the village. A relative, Osama El Najar, recalled that at 8 a.m. Israeli soldiers used megaphones to order the locals to congregate in the village centre. Rawhiah and Yasmin El Najar were the first to come out.

Yasmin, who survived the attack, remembered that other women came out of neighbouring houses. 'We all walked towards the centre waving white flags. I then saw a soldier pointing his gun towards us. I thought he was asking us to come closer; we continued to walk. Suddenly, he opened fire. I was hit in my right leg. Rawhiah was hit in the head. I tried to reach Rawhiah to help but the soldiers continued to shoot. They also shot at an ambulance driver who tried to reach her. He was forced to go back.' By the time the medical teams were allowed access, Rawhiah was already dead.

Schools and hospitals were also bombed. Al Fakhora School in Jabalia was one of three UN schools bombed by the Israeli army, although the UN had provided the army with co-ordinates of all its schools in the Gaza Strip. When the bombs hit Al Fakhora on 6 January hundreds of civilians were sheltering inside. Forty-five civilians were killed, dozens more injured (inside the school and in the neighbouring area).

The Israeli army also attacked Al Quds hospital, run by the Palestinian Red Crescent Society. This, too, was in clear violation of the fourth Geneva Convention. Images of medical staff rushing out of Al Quds hospital, pushing four incubators with four premature babies inside, were a shocking demonstration of how far the Israelis were prepared to go. Medical staff, as they were fleeing, had to manually pump oxygen to five intensive care patients. In total, fifteen hospital beds had to be removed from the severely damaged hospital.

The Israelis claimed after the bombing of the UN schools and Al Quds hospital that they were responding to firing from these two sites. Even if there was armed resistance close by, which has not been proven, this would not have made them legitimate targets under international law.

History repeated itself: Israel gave the same explanation following the Qana massacre in southern Lebanon, in 1996. Then, Israeli army shelling of a village close to a UN compound killed 100 civilians including a one-month-old baby. A year later, the UN report confirmed, at the time of the attack, there were no Hizbullah fighters in the area.

The use of civilians as human shields on many occasions during the attacks was documented by the Goldstone report and a plethora of other human rights organizations. During Operation Cast Lead the Israeli army arrested hundreds of civilians, subjected them to torture and interrogation and, in many cases, illegally tried them.

The attacks did not spare environmental targets. On the first day of the attacks, the Israeli air force bombed Al Nimir Water Wells Complex in Jabalia. The complex included two wells, pumps, generator, fuel store room, equipment and buildings. There was no evidence this complex was used by Palestinian armed groups. The bombing could not have been carried out by mistake given the size of the complex. The Israeli army gained no military advantage from the destruction. It was purely an act of collective punishment. The sewage treatment tanks in Gaza City were also bombed, resulting in the release of more than 200,000 cubic metres of untreated sewage into the adjacent agricultural land.

The destruction of Al Badir Flower Mill, the only working mill in the Gaza Strip, on 9 January 2009, was also a clear violation of the fourth Geneva Convention. The traffic officers killed on the first day of the Israeli attacks appear at first sight to have been a military target. According to the protocols of the Lahai Agreement of 1907, for an attack to be legitimate, it must be launched on a legitimate military target. The traffic officers were part of the Islamic Resistance movement's (Hamas) civilian police force and not its military wing. The criminalization and targeting of the traffic officers, according to the Israeli newspaper *Haretz*, was based on the assumption that it was a force likely to resist the invading Israeli army. This made them a legitimate target according to Israel but not according to international law.

These war crimes have, once again, exposed the hypocrisy of the US administration, the British government and the European Union. They failed, as in the past, to take any action to try to halt war crimes or to apply sanctions once they were committed. On the contrary, they blamed the Palestinians, claiming that, 'Israel, like any other Western democracy, cannot stand watching while rockets are launched into their innocent civilians.' This propaganda was ready even before the attack on Gaza. The truth is that, before the bloody Saturday of 27 December, the Israeli army had invaded the Gaza Strip twice on 5 and 18 November killing a total of 17 Palestinians, many of them civilians, and injuring many more. This was a clear violation of the six-month truce with Hamas which the Egyptians had brokered and which was due to end on 19 December. In response to Israel's violation of the truce, Hamas declared an end to it and launched a wave of rocket attacks on Israel.

Israel portrays Palestinian suicide bombings as driven by fanaticism, as irrational actions that are unrelated to its own actions. Yet almost every suicide bombing was preceded by an Israeli attack. This included the killing of Palestinian civilians, the collective destruction of Palestinian houses, wells, agricultural lands and extra-judicial targeted assassination of paramilitary leaders – most infamously, the assassination of the leader of al-Aqsa Martyrs Brigades in the West Bank, Raed Al Karmi, on 14 January 2002. This led to the end of the ceasefire which Yasser Arafat called upon all armed wings of Fateh to abide by and was implemented on 16 December 2001. As a result al-Aqsa Martyrs Brigades, the main military wing of Fateh, launched, for the first time in Fateh's history, a wave of suicide bombings inside the Green Line.

The same applies to the assassination of the leader of al-Qassam Brigades, the military wing of Hamas in Palestine, Salah Shihadah, on 23 July 2002. As a result of F16 jet fighters bombing his house, 16 people were killed, including nine children. This led to a wave of suicide bombings by Hamas. It was revealed afterwards, that at the same time as Shihada's assassination, the Egyptian government was secretly negotiating a ceasefire between Israel and the Palestinians. This ceasefire was supposed to include Hamas. All these efforts were destroyed by the assassination of Shihadah.

Nearly four years have passed since the start of the Operation Cast Lead. The damage caused by three weeks of war has yet to be repaired.

1

The apple of my eye

The sun disappeared behind the horizon on a typical warm Gaza December day. I had arrived at my family's house in Khan Younis following an unexpectedly easy journey through the Rafah Border Crossing.[1] The timing of my arrival was not intentional: but it was two weeks before the second anniversary of Operation Cast Lead.

---

[1] The Rafah Border Crossing lies on the international border between Egypt and the Gaza Strip recognized by the 1979 Israel-Egypt Peace Treaty. The crossing was managed by Israel until it evacuated Gaza on 11 September 2005 as part of Israel's unilateral disengagement plan. Control of the border corridor was handed over to the Palestinian National Authority under an agreement reached in November 2005.

Until July 2007, the Rafah Crossing was jointly controlled by Egypt and the Palestinian Authority, with the European Union Border Assistance Mission monitoring Palestinian compliance on the Gaza side. The border was regularly closed for long periods at Israeli orders, putting the entire population of the Gaza Strip under partial siege and leaving thousands of Palestinians stranded on both sides.

In June 2007, the Rafah Crossing was completely closed after the Hamas takeover of the Gaza Strip.

On 28 May 2010, was opened for Palestinians to cross into Egypt. Even though passenger restrictions were relaxed, a small number of Palestinians, approximately 300 daily, are allowed to travel to Egypt through the border. The shipment into Gaza of goods remains blocked.

I did not sleep well on that first night; I kept waking up thinking about whether I would be able to achieve what I came to Gaza for. It was a hugely emotional and intense mission – what if the families changed their minds and did not wish to meet me? And if they agreed, how was I going to be able to talk to them without breaking open their severe emotional wounds? What if they thought I was yet another person doing yet another report about their suffering as something for people to look at, feel sorry, then forget all about it? What, what, what, what . . . ?

The following morning the phone rang. It was Muhammad Al Majdalawi who had been working hard on arranging meetings with the families of the victims prior to my arrival. Muhammad gave me some good news: he had set up an interview with the Deeb family who lost 11 members at Jabalia refugee camp during the war.

I drove along Al Jalla'a Street leading out of Gaza City towards the north, to Jabalia refugee camp where Muhammad had arranged for me to meet the family. Almost everything in Gaza is named after a political figure or event. 'Al Jalla'a' in Arabic means the departure. The street was named after the 1954 'Jalla'a', the withdrawal of the British troops from Egypt, following the July 1952 revolution led by Jamal Abdul Nasser.

First-time visitors to the area would not realize how much it has changed. They might well think they were still in Gaza City though they had already arrived in Jabalia. This stretch of road is filled with new residential areas – contiguous concrete structures all the way along with barely any empty space in-between. This used to be one of the pretty parts of the Gaza Strip: orange groves; olive orchards and vineyards; a mixture of green and yellow sandy areas. It is heartbreaking to see all that buried by concrete. Population increase has turned the Gaza Strip into one of the most heavily populated areas in the world, forcing Gazans to build on agricultural land. Long decades of Israeli occupation have contributed substantially to a severe lack of proper town planning.

Jabalia camp is one of the biggest refugee camps in the Gaza Strip, sheltering 130,000 Palestinians, mostly second and third generation refugees whose parents and grandparents were forcibly uprooted by Zionist militias attacks during the 1948 war. In 2006 in Jabalia, I was fortunate to meet Hajja Tamam, a 78-year-old Palestinian woman from Beit Jirja village inside the Green Line.[2] Om Tamam was 20 in 1948 when the Nakba happened.[3]

---

[2] Beit Jirja, 15.5 kilometres north-east of Gaza, was occupied on 30 October 1948. The village was completely destroyed by the Zionist militias in 1948 – only one house out of 202 remains. Over a thousand inhabitants were completely ethnically cleansed. (www.Palestineremembered.com)

[3] 'Nakba' means 'catastrophe' in Arabic. It refers to the destruction of Palestinian society in 1948 when more than 725,000 Palestinians – approximately two-thirds of the Palestinian population – were forced into exile by Zionist militias. More than 50 per cent fled under direct military assault. Others fled in panic at news of massacres committed by Zionist militias.

More than 450 Palestinian towns and villages were demolished to prevent the return of the refugees. (Figures for the number of towns and villages destroyed and depopulated by the Zionist militias vary. The Israeli daily newspaper *Ha'aretz* reports 530 lost villages.) These comprised three-quarters of the Palestinian villages inside the areas held by Israeli forces after the end of the war. The newly established Israeli government confiscated refugees' land and properties and turned them over to Jewish immigrants. The pre-1948 Jewish population of Palestine represented 33 per cent of the total population. This percentage rose from 7 per cent at the turn of the twentieth century as a result of waves of Jewish immigrants arriving in Palestine following the Balfour declaration of 2 November 1917, which promised the establishment of a homeland for the Jews in Palestine. Israel was established on 78 per cent of Palestine. Until the present day Israel has disregarded the right of return for the Palestinian refugees.

The expulsion of the Palestinians has been described by the renowned Israeli historian, Professor Ilan Pappe, as ethnic cleansing (*The Ethnic Cleansing of Palestine*, London: Oneworld, 2007). In his address to the Technion, Haifa (Israel Institute of Technology) (as quoted in *Ha'aretz*, 4 April 1969), Moshe Dayan, a former Israeli defence minister said: 'Jewish

As her two grandchildren, Majd and Shahd, with their cousin Rawan (members of Al Asria folk dance group) performed an impromptu Palestinian folk dance, she said, 'This is good but nothing compared to how I used to dance in weddings when I was their age. I was so much more energetic; I used to jump up and down like a monkey.'

She recalled the Nakba tearfully: the horrific period when her village came under attack. 'They fired on our village day and night. The airplanes started to drop Qeezan [a tankful of explosives]. Many villagers were killed or injured as a result. The Egyptian army unit based outside our village withdrew to Gaza. After that people decided to leave. We started walking, carrying what we could and leaving almost everything behind. We thought that this was a nightmare which will end soon; there is no way that the world will allow such a tragedy to happen. We were wrong.

'At night we hid under orange trees on the road to Gaza. We couldn't use white covers as we were worried the airplane would see them and bomb us. We arrived in Gaza hungry and exhausted. Tens of thousands of refugees from different towns and villages in Palestine had already arrived, more arrived later. We lived on the streets for a few weeks; luckily enough it was warm during May 1948. We were given food by the United Nations; locals also helped us.

'After a time they moved us to a camp built by the UN which was surrounded by barbed wires. My family was allocated a tent, it was awful. We were crammed next to each other for months. There were few communal toilets in the camp; I always had to queue to go to the toilets. We also queued for food. It was humiliating. A few months later the UN built different camps to accommodate the

---

(cont.) villages were built in the place of Arab villages. You do not even know the names of these Arab villages, and I do not blame you because geography books no longer exist, not only do the books not exist, the Arab villages are not there either. There is not one single place built in this country that did not have a former Arab population.' (www.thepalestineyoudontknow.tumblr.com, www.imeu.net, www.Palestine-remembered.com)

large number of refugees. We were allocated a small house in Jabalia refugee camp. Initially there were no toilets inside any of the camp houses. We continued to queue for toilets until things got better.

'Now, after 58 years of Nakba, my kids worked hard and we managed to build this house.' Hajja Tamam sighed as she remembered the trauma of visiting her three political-prisoner sons, who were in different Israeli prisons. 'Not only did we lose everything during the Nakba but I lived to see my sons denied their freedom. I love Gaza but no place will ever be as good as Beit Jirja. I make sure that I tell all my grandchildren and their friends about our village and the good life we had pre-1948. I have not forgotten and I am sure that they will not either.'

Another member of Al Asria folk dance group was Mustafa Awadh. I met his father Muhammad who told me a shocking story about his family's flight from their village, Burayr.[4] Muhammad was one month old; the village was under fierce attack by the Zionist militias; there was panic. His family ran for their lives. Four hours on the road to Gaza and utterly traumatized, they realized they had left baby Muhammad behind. His father, at the risk of being killed, went back to fetch him. By then, Muhammad was screaming inconsolably. Muhammad, to this day, does not understand how his family could have left him behind. 'I kept saying to my parents, when they were alive, how could you? They always said that they had no excuse but I know how much they loved me and I realized what a horrific experience they had to have gone through to leave me behind. I always laughed with them, saying I forgive them.'

I arrived at Al Fakhoura square at the top of the cul-de-sac where the extended Deeb family home is located. Mu'in Deeb was waiting for me. At the entrance stands a massive poster with photos in remembrance of the 11 civilian victims of the Deeb family killed by

---

[4] Burayr is 18 kilometres north-east of Gaza. The village was occupied by the Zionist Giv'ati Brigade on 12 May 1948. It was completely destroyed: only house rubble left behind. Some village streets are still visible. Burayr's 3175 inhabitants were completely ethnically cleansed. (www.Palestineremembered.com)

an Israeli missile. It was summer 2008. Mu'in Deeb remembered: 'I was very happy. Our extended family together with our late beloved mother Shammah went to the beach as we did every summer. I still remember the joy we had on that day. My youngest, my 4-year-old daughter Noor in her yellow swimming costume playing with her 9-year-old sister Asil; her wide eyes shining with excitement. Asil and Noor built sandcastles and enjoyed themselves. They played with their brothers and sister Alla'a and their cousins. No one realized this would be their last chance to visit the beach.

'Our house is only 100 metres from Al Fakhoura, the UN school in Jabalia refugee camp,' Mu'in said. 'Five thousand civilians were seeking shelter in the school. They fled their homes in Al Attattra area where the Israeli ground attack stated. They thought their area to be safe as it is at least two kilometres from the ground attack. They were so terrified that they left all their belongings behind. They had only the clothes they were wearing.'

Mu'in remembered how the family used to gather in the front yards of the houses of extended family. 'We were always around my mother Hajja Shammah; she was kind, she gave everyone around her comfort and confidence. As the shelling and shooting continued day and night, my mother tried her best to make everyone around her escape the horrors of the reality of the situation, especially the children. My father was originally from Yibna village,[5] my mother was from Wadi Hunain village,[6] both inside the

---

[5] The village of Yibna was located 15 kilometres south-west of Al Ramla, near Ben Gurion Airport. Yibna was occupied by the Zionist militias on 4 June 1948. It was mostly destroyed with the exception of two houses and the village mosque. Yibna's entire Palestinian population of 6,287 were ethnically cleansed. All of them fled to the Gaza Strip. (www.Palestineremembered.com)

[6] The village of Wadi Hunain was located 9 kilometres west of Al Ramla, near Ben Gurion Airport. It was occupied by the Zionist militias on 17 April 1948. It was virtually destroyed with the exception of a few houses and a mosque which is now functioning as a synagogue. The entire 1,879-strong Palestinian population of the village was ethnically cleansed. (www.Palestineremembered.com)

Green Line. She was 73 years old. My mother thought in the days before she was killed that the 1948 Nakba was happening again.

Mu'in's younger brother Hussain started telling me what he remembers of that horrific day. 'We were in the front yard. It happened at approximately 3.30 p.m. on 6 January 2009 during the truce which was declared by the Israeli army. Minutes before, Asil and Noor were fighting over a silly thing so we split them apart and were laughing.

'Suddenly there was a massive noise and the atmosphere was filled with dust. My nieces Alla'a and Fatima were preparing the dough inside the front room. Suddenly one shell hit the orange grove next to the house. We thought it was a mistake. The children started screaming; we tried our best to calm them down. Another shell fell near the orchard. Moments later a further shell landed in the middle of us. Thick black smoke covered the scene; the smell was disgusting, it was like a nightmare. When the smoke bombs were launched on us we thought that this is the end; it felt like real clouds very close to you. I was among the less badly injured. I carried my niece Noor away from the scene and passed her to first aid helpers. Her wounds were too severe and she died. My injuries prevented me from helping anyone else,' Hussain sighed.

Hussain insisted on telling me how the investigators from the Israeli Human Rights Organization B'Tselem and the Red Cross were shocked at the amount of shrapnel that came off the rocket which caused their family's tragedy.

Mu'in was away from home at the time of the shelling but had seen the shells landing near there and could see large numbers of injured and dead being ferried to hospital. 'I rushed home; most of the injured and dead had been taken to Kamal Odwan Hospital. There I learned that my mother, Shammah, wife, Amal, who was three months pregnant, and daughters, Asil and Noor, my sons Mustafa, 14, and Muhammad, 16, had all been killed. My brother, Samir, was also killed in the attack; as were my nephews, Muhammad, 24, Isam, 14, and niece Fatima, 21. My other nephew, Ziad Samir Deeb, was hit by shrapnel. Both his legs and one hand were amputated. His brother Fadel emerged physically well but the sight of the carnage in the courtyard sent him into a state of shock from which he still suffers.'

Fadel told me how loving and caring his father and brothers were. 'My brother Ziyad suffers from severe disability. I suddenly found myself responsible for everything when I was supposed to be building my future. I was hoping to start my life but suddenly everything was taken away from me,' he sighed with visible sadness.

Mu'in recalls these horrific moments. 'Four of my kids died instantly. Alla'a was severely injured. Her injury was all over the right side of her body. Alla'a was moved to the Intensive Care Unit in Al Ahli Bank hospital in Egypt. She was in a coma almost all the time. She woke up for few hours only. Once at hospital the nurse came to me asking: "Is your daughter studying for her second year at university?" I was ecstatic – this meant she had become conscious. I asked her to answer me with signs. I asked her: "Do you know what happened? No? Do you know where you are?" She replied, "No." I lied to her: I told her that all the family were fine, nothing wrong. I wiped her head; I prayed for her and asked her to pray. I wanted to leave but she pulled at my hand implying that I should not leave. I stayed longer until she fell back into a coma. I was praying all the time that she will live so that my only remaining son, Bakir, will have a sister and she will have a brother, after I had already lost four children. The procedure to move her to Egypt contributed to her deterioration. We moved by land. It was a ten-hour journey. I started preparing papers so that a Medical Human Rights delegation will take her to France. I was ready to sell my house and everything to pay for her treatment but it was not meant to be. She died after two days. She died as a result of a shrapnel wound near her hip which raised her temperature to above 40.

'Noor was the apple of my eye. If you see any videos of her, you will realize how lovely she was. She was so special, she was the youngest. My daughter Asil was very clever at school, she was so dear to me. She always laughed and joked. She was always chosen for activities around school. Asil was very popular with everyone young and old. She loved painting. Her handwriting was outstanding. She was very scared of punishment when she was mischievous; she used to hide under her bed when she did something wrong.

'Mustafa, my 14-year-old son, was very funny, very popular; we miss him. His grandmother would not go anywhere without taking him with her. Even in her death she took him with her. He loved to impersonate other people and make us laugh. He kept adding jokes in his book. Mustafa and his cousin Isam, Samir's son, were very good friends. Everyone called them the twins, they were inseparable. How tragic for both of them to die at the same time, as if they were meant never to be separated.

'I am a good cook, my wife and I used to cook together. My kids would wait for me to eat with them. They loved food. Our atmosphere was a family one; our life was so lovely together. What happened destroyed everything. It would take a lifetime for me to get back to normal. I do not think that it ever will.

'We all keep remembering Noor and Asil when we look at their school books which I kept and their toys and teddies. Noor had her own Palestinian flag and kuffiyah.

'Asil, Mustafa, Isam and Muhammad always took part in peaceful demonstrations against the brutality of the Israeli occupation army; they loved candlelit vigils. Thinking back, they were protesting about something that they thought may happen to them and it did.

'Every minute of every day is suffering, if for a moment I forget Asil, I remember Alla'a, Mustafa or Muhammad who should have been in his first year at university.

'I was working but now I have asked for early retirement. I can't continue to work after what has happened, there is nothing for me to live for. Every day, I wish I would die. My only remaining son, Bakir, who is 21 years old, has got married and is independent now.

'We are waiting and anticipating. We hope one day we will be able to testify to the whole world about the crime that was committed against us. This household strongly believes in peace but what happened to us changes your view of life. The Zionists do not believe in peace, they are killers. They think that they are a cut above the rest of humanity. I feel outraged when I see photos of Israeli children writing hate messages on the rockets ready to be launched against us, like the one which caused our tragedy.

'What happened makes me realize that the only way for the Israelis to understand the severity of our pain is for them to experience something similar. This is not the real me talking, this is the victim of brutality.

'We were comforted by others. A lot of people suggested that we have psychological treatment. But after what happened all the Palestinian people need psychological treatment.'

2

A boy, a dog and a broken cage

I left the Deeb family home to meet Ahmad Qartam's family: Ahmad was a 9-year-old child killed in the attacks. Their house is very close to Kamal Odwan hospital[7] in Jabalia. This hospital, and the Al Awda hospital in Jabalia, were overwhelmed by the large number of casualties from the Israeli attacks on the north of the Gaza Strip.

At the peak of the Israeli attack on Gaza, there was a strange scratching noise at the main door of the Qartam family house on Al Yarmouk Street in Gaza City. Osama was worried. He opened the door reluctantly. A dog was standing outside. As he told it to leave, his son Ahmad clung to his leg and begged him not to. He said the dog was his.

'What do you mean it is yours?' said Osama. 'I can't recall you having a dog.'

'I used part of my pocket money to buy food for the dog which was wandering in the neighbourhood,' Ahmad replied. 'I kept him on a nearby plot of land because I was worried what you and mother would say.' Osama laughed. He was touched by this and allowed Ahmad to keep the dog under the staircase in front of the house.

---

[7] Kamal Odwan was a member of the central committee for the Fateh organization. He was assassinated by the Israeli special units in 1973 together with his colleagues Kamal Nassir and Abu Youssef Al-Najjar in Beirut. Many members of their families and neighbours were killed and injured in the attack.

Osama related to me, 'On 15 January 2009, at 4 p.m., Israeli F16 jet fighters shelled the Sa'adieh family's house, near ours, in which Sayed Siyam, the Hamas minister of the interior, was hiding. Many children were playing in front of the house. The shelling destroyed the house, killing those inside. My neighbour Saber Abu Aisheh's family house was also hit in the same attack. The house was destroyed, killing Saber, his wife and three children and wounding many people in the neighbourhood.

'We had been in front of our house on a piece of land which belongs to us. It is just across from Sa'adieh's house. Suddenly there was a massive explosion; the air was full of dust and black stones were falling. Ahmad and his friend Zuhair were playing in front of us with the dog. Shrapnel and debris were flying everywhere. Ahmad was killed by a reinforced concrete pillar falling on him. I went to help him. I noticed the back of his head was open. His brains fell into my hand. Zuhair was badly wounded. He needed 150 surgical stitches to treat his injury. Many of the children playing with him were wounded. My baby daughter Farah was 14 months old at the time. She was breast-feeding when suddenly she was thrown in the air. We could not find where she was for a while. We found her hanging onto the window rails, safe and sound. We are extremely fortunate that she did not suffer any permanent brain damage.

'Our house was badly damaged. People came from everywhere. Sometimes I do not know how I kept my sanity after carrying his brains in my hand.

'When we brought Ahmad's body back, his dog sat next to the body for hours refusing to eat or drink. It looked sad. Afterwards, the dog disappeared for three days then came back, but it did not look normal. We gave it food and drink; a few hours later, it climbed on top of a pile of aggregates and died. It was heartrending for all of us; the bond between this dog and Ahmad was so strong that it could not live after Ahmad died.

'We had to move to this rented accommodation because my daughter Fatima, 8, is still traumatized by the incident. I have four daughters and two sons. Fatima has been the most affected. For months she could not talk, she was not able to urinate. She had to have medical help. Just today I took her to the psychiatrist. Sometimes she seems to be fine; after a while she will start biting her brothers and sisters, fighting with them. She saw her brother Ahmad being cut to pieces and covered in blood. She took some of my money to school; she started distributing it to her classmates. The school's headteacher phoned and my wife went to get the money. The medicines affect her badly and she suffers regular nightmares and night time incontinence. We have lost the feeling of happiness. Ahmad was my first child. I used to say only the father and mother of any victim will feel the pain and sorrow of the loss of a loved one. Now I am going through the same feelings and emotions.

'Ahmad loved birds. I once got him a bird in a cage. The following morning, Ahmad broke the cage and set the bird free: he told me that he couldn't bear the sad look in the bird's eyes. He also loved horses and dogs.

'Sometimes when I see his photos I get very upset. When he finished at the Space Toon Nursery, the graduation ceremony was very nice. He looked adorable. I now see graduation ceremonies for children and cry. I imagine Ahmad is one of them. They burned our hearts. I once told his mother, "One day our hardship will ease when Ahmad graduates from university and starts helping us." They denied us all this.

'I'm sorry that I don't want you to talk about all this with my wife, Ghada. If you did, she would not sleep for days. She suffered a stroke after Ahmad's death. At the first day of the feast of Eid, I went out to buy stuff for the family. I could not bear it. Ahmad always came with me. I went back and asked my wife to go instead. When a customer next to her asked for clothes for her son who was Ahmad's age Ghada had a nervous breakdown. We took her to hospital where she stayed for a few days. Ramadan is not the same. We do not feel happy at all.

'The day he was killed he asked for *ijja* [omlette]. We are not able to eat this meal any more.

'We refused to wrap his body in any organization's flag. He was an innocent child, a child of Palestine and he was wrapped in the Palestinian flag. We buried him next to his grandmother.

'Ironically Ahmad will be added to the list of martyrs in our family. Three of my brothers were killed by the Israelis. Abdul Qadir and Abdul Rahman were killed in the 1948 Nakba in Al Masmiyah, where we originally came from.[8] In 1969 Yousif was killed by the Israelis in Gaza City. He was an 11-year-old child. My father soon followed him.

'I have other brothers whom I am also very proud of. One of my brothers was one of the first Palestinian teachers. One of his sons is a specialist cardiologist in the USA.

'I will continue with my family to campaign until these criminals who killed my son are brought to justice. Also those who support the Zionists are guilty. They are like Nazis. They have no humanity. I want to ask the Israeli defence minister "What did all these children who were savagely killed do to the Israelis?" Was my 8-year-old child carrying a gun when he and others like him were killed? What type of democracy do they talk about? They are killers. We want the whole world to see the crimes of the Zionists.'

As I was leaving the Qartam family home, Ahmad's 3-year-old brother Mahmoud insisted on adding something. 'My brother Ahmad was killed by the Israelis. When I grow up I will kill all who killed him.' Ahmad's other brother, 4-year-old Abdul Qader, said brother Ahmad was put in Paradise.

---

[8] Al Masmiyah village is 41 kilometres north-east of Gaza. It was occupied by the Zionist militias on 8 July 1948. Its 2,923 Palestinian inhabitants were completely ethnically cleansed. The village has been mostly destroyed apart from its two schools and several houses which remain standing. The girls' school is deserted while the boys' school has been converted into an Israeli army installation.

3

I talk to him for hours then I sneak back in

A few hundred metres to the east of the Qartam family we were received by Ribhi Eid and his wife Tahani at their house at Al Mahkama Street. When Tahani realized we wanted to talk to her about her late son Mustafa she erupted in a flood of non-stop crying for a good quarter of an hour. 'Do people still remember my Mustafa?' We waited while her husband and sons comforted her. It was agonizing to watch.

Adjacent to their house is a grocery shop owned by a relative, Hamed Abed Rabu. The shop has been open for several decades and functions as a meeting point, as in many neighbourhoods. People will buy what they need and linger outside the shop to socialize for a while before going back to their homes. This is exactly what they were doing on 10 January 2009 when the Israeli army declared a truce. Almost everyone in their street came out. Tahani (45) recalled, 'I was on my way to Hamed's grocery shop near our house at around 11.30 in the morning. There was a drone in the air but people believed in the Israeli army truce. I suddenly heard an explosion. A rocket was fired from a drone not far from me.

'I ran to the location approximately 20 metres away. I saw a number of people lying on the ground in the middle of the road. Seven were killed.[9] My son Mustafa who was 19 and my 35-year-old

[9] Muhammad Mustafa Ribhi Abdel Khalek Hussain Eid, Yusri Mahmoud Jawdat Abed Rabu, Sufian Abdel Hay Jawdat Abed Rabu, Randa Jamal Faraj Abed Rabu, Ramez Jamal Abed Rabu, Sami Abed Rabu and Samed Abed Rabu. (Al Dameer Association for Human Rights, Gaza)

brother Sami Abed Rabu were among the dead. The ambulances could not get to the scene because the occupation forces which were at the nearby Izbit Abed Rabu neighbourhood would not allow them to reach the injured and killed. They were carried on the shoulders of neighbours. Some were transferred on a cart pulled by a donkey until they could reach the ambulances that were waiting at Al Jurn roundabout, about a kilometre away, and were then transferred to Kamal Odwan hospital. None of them belonged to any organization. All the dead were unarmed civilians and there were no fighters or armed men at the scene.'

The shop owner, Hamed, who was injured in the attack recalls: 'I was inside the shop. There were 12 neighbours and relatives sitting under the shop's concrete canopy. My shop was nearly empty and I was preparing to buy supplies. Suddenly a rocket fell from a drone in the midst of those by the entrance, and shrapnel hit different parts of my body.'

'On the morning of that terrible day Mustafa had his breakfast. He made everyone coffee as he always did,' Tahani continued. 'He was still in his pyjamas. He said, "Mum, there is a truce and I want to go to the shop." I told him, "You can never trust the Israeli army." He laughed and said, "Do not worry Mum, I will be alright." That was the last thing he said to me.

'Mustafa came to me days before he was killed. He told me that his friend Belal had been killed, he was sobbing loudly and his face was red. He wanted to go to the funeral but I tried to stop him. He begged me to let him go to say his last farewell and, in the end, I let him go.

'I used to feel sad for the suffering of any Israeli mothers and I never hesitated to say so. But I feel they killed this feeling inside me after taking my Mustafa away from me forever. I would love to sit with a group of mothers of Israeli soldiers and ask them: How do you feel after your son killed my beloved Mustafa? I really would love to do that. I just want to tell them that I was a very happy and fit mother who devoted her entire life to her kids. How did I end up as a result of their kids' actions? A physical and psychological wreck. Would they understand? I don't think so. They would not understand my pain unless they experienced something similar. In a way I think that it is only those who cause other people such an immense pain who should suffer the same. They do not feel our pain; they are very powerful; they don't regard us as equal to them. Sometimes I do not blame people who turned extremist; after all what have the Israelis done to us or offered us? Suffering and destruction, generation after generation. If they claim that they are for democracy and freedom, then why did they kill my innocent son?

'It is not something that happened and is over. It hurts me a lot that I feel that Mustafa has been forgotten. If he was a member of any of the resistance organizations; if he was a criminal who was found guilty of a crime that deserves capital punishment, then maybe I would tolerate the pain of losing him. I challenge any Israeli leader to bring me evidence to justify their attack on our street. If they can prove that there has been an attack on them from our area, then I will shut up.

'What can I say? I am his mother and I loved him so I will say good things about him. But if you ask other people they will tell you the same about him. One of our neighbours once told me that Mustafa was so charismatic that when you planned to see him for ten minutes you would end up talking to him for three hours without realizing the time.

'He loved his father and understood the hardship that we are going through. He always told me: "Mum, please don't upset my father. He is not earning much at the moment. Please do not ask him for any extra things. We do not want to make him feel inadequate."

'I have really lost the will to live. All I hope for is to die and be with Mustafa. I know this is selfish and hard on the rest of my kids and my husband but what can I do, this is how I feel. I try to resist this feeling but always fail.

'I asked for a meeting with my family and my husband's. I demanded that they find another wife for my husband. I am not fit enough to be a wife any more. Ribhy refused and told me to stop this because he does not want any other wife but me. I think that this is unfair on him.

'I have received a lot of psychiatric treatment but I am not improving. One of the psychiatrists was strict with me telling me sternly: "Do you think that you are the only one who lost a son?" I was very upset but then I realized he meant well by bringing to my attention that there are so many other people who are in my situation, if not worse. This did improve the way I felt for a while but then I was back to feeling the same.'

'Mustafa used to play tricks on me all the time,' Ribhy recalled. 'Once he sent a relative to me to ask me to get him married. I was surprised at the request but the man told me that this is Mustafa's request, not his. I did not know what to do because Mustafa was young and we cannot afford to get him married. After days of thinking long and hard about this, Mustafa came to me laughing his head off: "Daddy, I got you, didn't I?" It was all a joke.'

'I mourn not only the loss of my son Mustafa but also my beloved brother Sami who died in the same attack.

'I used to go to Mustafa's grave every day but my husband and family stopped me. They were worried my situation would continue to deteriorate. I pretended I accepted that but I regularly sneak out of the house after midnight without anyone knowing and go to Mustafa's grave.

'I was there when they buried him. I jumped into the grave and spent three hours hugging his body. I just wanted to be buried with him. I can never forget one evening when Mustafa came to me with tears in his eyes. He was holding his injured little kitten. It was hit in the street by a passing car. He spent all night nursing it. He wanted me to stay up with him and I did. The kitten died at about four in the morning. He cried a lot, brought a towel, wrapped the kitten in it and buried it under a tree in the front yard of our house. He was upset for weeks.

'I am convinced a major war will erupt as a result of Israeli crimes. After what they did to us in Gaza in the latest war, I think they are capable of doing anything even using their nuclear bombs. You may think this is a broken mother speaking out of her pain but this is the truth.'

4

For months we thought she was still with us

Across the road from the Eid family is the Abed Rabu sprawling family home. The family suffered great losses in the same attack on Hamed's grocery shop.

The name 'Abed Rabu' is associated with Izbit Abed Rabu which lies on a hill looking over Jabalia town and camp to the east. 'Izbit' in Arabic means a very small village. It was named after the Abed Rabu family. It has become notorious in the last decade. It was always the first stop for the Israeli army in their frequent invasions of the northern part of the Gaza Strip following the outburst of the second Palestinian *Intifada* in 2000. The Israeli army used Izbit Abed Rabu to place their tanks which then launched attacks on Jabalia and Beit Lahia. The area suffered much devastation in those years. Many inhabitants of Izbit Abed Rabu have either been killed or severely injured as a result. It was before one of the attacks on the village in 2008 when the deputy defence minister, Matan Vilnai, said the increased rocket fire by Palestinian militants would trigger what he called a 'bigger holocaust' in the Hamas-controlled coastal strip.

According to the BBC on 29 February 2008 this statement caused widespread shock and absolute horror. In the aftermath of the worldwide controversy Vilnai tried to issue a denial by saying Reuters news agency had mistranslated the word *Shoah* which means 'disaster' rather than 'holocaust'. The Israeli spin machine called this the mother of all mistranslations. However, this is contrary to the translation of 'Shoah' in most dictionaries.

The Israeli invasion following Vilnai's controversial statement started at dawn on 28 February 2008. It was one of the worst attacks the eastern part of Jabalia, including Izbit Abed Rabu, experienced. The Israeli army used tanks, F16 jet fighters, helicopters and infantry. The invading forces occupied the tops of many houses in Izbit Abed Rabu to use them as sniper platforms to fight against Hamas and other resistance fighters. They imprisoned entire families in one room for four days and destroyed furniture and possessions.

One of the houses occupied by the Israeli army belonged to the Kanan Tobail family. On 1 March 2008, across the road from the Tobails, 14-year-old Iyad Abu Shbak was in his kitchen when he was hit by a bullet fired by a sniper on top of the Tobail house. He went down screaming. His 16-year-old sister, Jacklene, was helping him when she was hit by another sniper bullet in the chest. Jacklene died instantly while Iyad died later in hospital.

Their mother, who was hiding at the time to protect her younger child, entered a state of shock and could not talk for a few weeks after the incident.

On the same day, near Izbit Abed Rabu, a 2-year-old toddler, Salsabil Abu Jalhoom, was playing in the front yard of her home with her brothers and sisters when they were hit by an Israeli tank shell. Salsabil died in hospital half an hour later. One of the most shocking tragedies of this invasion was the killing of four children hit by Israeli shells while playing football in Al Qirim Street, east of Jabalia.[10] The bodies, cut to pieces, were so mutilated that Naiem Hamouda, one of the fathers, could not decide which was his son.

In four days, the Israeli army killed 108 Palestinians, of whom 54 were civilians, including 26 children. This attack is commonly referred to by local Palestinians as *Al Mahraqa*, the 'Holocaust'.

Abdel Hai Abed Rabu received me; he was keen to tell me the story of his loss. 'My wife, Randa, said, "Since it is ceasing fire, let's get

[10] Muhammad Naiem Hamouda (9), Ali Munier Dardounah (8), Dardounah Deeb Dardounah (12) and Omar Hussain Dardounah (14) (PCHR).

out and buy some groceries." We went out with my son Sufian and my nephew Yosri. Some cousins were already at the entrance of Hamed's grocery shop. Sufian insisted on treating his mother Randa to a bar of chocolate. He went inside the shop, came out, opened the wrapper and started to pretend to feed Randa as if she were a little toddler. We were laughing; they felt like happy moments. Suddenly there was a loud explosion. All I can remember is being thrown in the air and then hitting the ground hard. Sufian did not realize that these chocolate bars would be the last he and Randa would ever have. Both were killed along with my nephew Yosri and four others. When neighbours found Randa's body, half of the chocolate bar was still in her mouth.'

Randa's sister, Halima, (64) cannot remember her younger sister without crying. I had to comfort her and wait until she was able to speak.

'We were four sisters. I am the eldest of the sisters. She was 44 years old. She was the best; you may think that I will say so and that is how people remember the loved ones when they pass away but this is really true. All through the war she was the bravest; she tried her best to keep our moral high. She is such a great loss – not only to us, her family, but to the entire neighbourhood. Everyone says they do not like to come to this house anymore since she is not here. She was the most welcoming, the warmest and the most hospitable.

'Once, some of our relatives fled their house at Izbit Abed Rabu which was under Israeli attack. They did not take anything with them other than the clothes which they were wearing. They came to Randa. "We need some clothes," they said. She gave them everything: food, clothes and soap. I did not live in this house during the war. When my grandson Nadir was killed by the Israelis during the attacks Randa insisted on coming to stand by us despite the great danger. She cooked a lot of food and brought it with her; it was enough for everyone in our household. I asked her why she had come; she could have been killed herself. She said, "Do not be silly, how I can leave you in times like these?"

'Everyone ran away when the Israeli army attacked the area with white phosphorus on the night of 9 October 2009. Randa refused. She said, "I will not leave my house, no matter what." We came back the following morning. I told you she was the bravest didn't I?

'She was very kind to her grandchildren. Two hours before she was killed, she fed her grandson Ghassan and asked her daughter-in-law Sabrin to wrap him in an extra blanket. She always checked on all members of the family before going to bed. Ghassan was named after his dad who was killed in *Al Mahraqah* [the Holocaust] in 2008. He was a member of a resistance group.'

'We had four sons,' Abdul Hai sighed. 'Sufian and Ghassan were married the same day. It was one of the happiest days of our life. Randa sang and danced all night long.'

'My kids were traumatized when I remarried, they could not bear the idea of someone replacing their mother. My 20-year-old son, Basim, was the most traumatized; he had been his mother's favourite.'

'My mother loved me more than any of my brothers,' Basim recalled. 'This caused a lot of friction in the family but my mother could not hide how much she favoured me.'

'After the death of Ghassan in *Al Mahraqa*, my mother asked me to marry his widow. I know that to many people this may sound a bit backward but to my mother and to me this was a way to protect Ghassan's kids and his wife by keeping the family together and it is working out well. We are happy together and I love my nephews. My brother Muhammad also married Sufian's widow and they are happy together. My mother keeps appearing in my dreams; three or four times weekly. She always asks me to look after Ghassan's kids.

'She had a good sense of humor. She loved to crack jokes. She always played tricks on everyone; she was very cheeky in a nice way. She hated bad times, or people who brought bad news.

'We could not believe the shock: for months and months we thought she was still with us. It was unbelievable; she was only in the grocery shop trying to buy some food for us.'

'They engraved hatred in our hearts,' Basim continued. 'If someone kills one of your pets you feel outraged, how about losing two brothers and a very dear mother?'

Abdul Hai's brother Mahmoud sat next to him listening. His 20-year-old son Yosri was killed in the same attack. Mahmoud, who was injured, remembers with noticeable pride: 'Yosri was the one who extinguished the fires when we were hit with white phosphorus on Friday night, a day before he was killed. He did not care about the raging fires; he just braved his way to help.

'We did not expect the Israeli army to be so vicious against civilians. There was no resistance from our neighbourhood.'

5

Gaza: the contrast

Meeting Mustafa's mother Tahani was one of the most painful experiences of my mission. Seeing the Abed Rabus had only compounded that feeling. I felt completely drained of energy. I could not even contemplate the half-hour drive to my family home in Khan Younis. I decided to stay the night at my sister Mona's house in Gaza. I got up in the morning ready to visit the Shbair family.

Driving west on Omar Al Mukhtar Street towards the Mediterranean, I entered the relatively affluent Rimal area. There were smart-looking buildings, wide streets, elegant boutiques, cafés, and expensive restaurants, some offering French, Italian or Thai cuisine. Looking at the surroundings, for a while, you feel it's like any other capital in the Arab world. At Al Rimal a person can go horse riding, play tennis in three different places, hire a chalet with a swimming pool, or have piano or violin lessons. There are private schools including an American one. Yet in the Gaza Strip the consequences of the 1948 Nakba cannot be forgotten. Painful reminders are everywhere.

At the top of Omar Al Mukhtar Street the taxi turned right and within a few hundred metres the picture before me had changed completely. We had entered the beach refugee camp, Al Shati. The narrow alleys with washing lines outside most of the houses give an indication of how crowded and poor this area is, like most neighbourhoods in the Gaza Strip. The Shbair family lived in the beach camp. The family had fled their village, Hamama, inside the Green Line, escaping with their lives from the Zionist militia attacks.[11] Over 60 years later, they are still in the same refugee camp, dreaming of the day they can return to Hamama.

Kamal Shbair and his wife Om Yassir received me at the front of their house with welcoming smiles.

'My son Yassir was 23 years old,' Kamal said while serving us tea and biscuits. 'He was working as a paramedic nurse at the Ministry of Health in Gaza. He worked for Al Masrooji pharmaceutical company for a while. They offered him a permanent position. But he wanted to work in nursing, the field he loved more than any other profession.'

Kamal told me how Yassir's colleague Hazem Al-Barrawi, an ambulance driver, remembered the last minutes of Yassir's life. 'Hazim and Yassir responded on 4 January 2009, around 3.30 p.m., to an emergency call from Tal Al-Hawa, Al Dahadeeh Street number 10. They went to the location. There were four in the ambulance: Hazim, Yassir, and two volunteers, Anas Naiem and Ra'fat Abdul Al, who were both 25 years old. On their arrival, they found a terrible scene. A young boy was shouting hysterically while pointing to where the casualties were. Hazim was driving the ambulance. The three paramedics, including Yassir, got out of the ambulance carrying stretchers to pick up the casualties. Hazim turned the ambulance round so they could put the injured on board. The driver of another ambulance shouted that the wheels of Hazim's ambulance were spinning in place. Hazim opened the door and got out to check. Suddenly, there was a loud explosion behind the ambulance. All Hazim could see was dust and blackness where the explosion had been. He started to call Yassir and his colleagues. When the dust settled he saw their torn bodies. He ran towards the other ambulance and another missile was launched into the area where he was standing. A 12-year-old child called

---

[11] Hamama village was located 24 kilometres north-east of Gaza. It was occupied by the Zionist Giva'ti Brigade on 4 November 1948. In 1945 the population of Hamama was 5,070, out of which 60 were Jewish. The village was completely obliterated in 1948 and all its 5,812 Palestinian inhabitants were ethnically cleansed. All the refugees from Hamama fled to the Gaza Strip. (www.Palestineremembered.com)

Omar Al Baradi was also killed in the attack. An hour later, a paramedic team including Hazim went back to the scene in one of the Palestinian Red Crescent ambulances. They brought back the bodies of his two colleagues, Yassir and Anas Naiem.

'The ambulance was clearly marked with the Ministry of Health Logo and lots of yellow and red florescent stripes. It was crystal clear it was nothing but an ambulance.'

Yassir's mother Om Yassir recalled, 'He was with me before he went on his mission. It was the first time in his life he asked everyone to forgive him, as if he knew that he would die. He was on his way out to work. I was worried because he had two briefcases with the First Aid medical supplies in them; he always carried them around. I was worried the Israelis would kill him. I brought two bin liners and asked him to put the briefcases inside. He laughed and said, "Do you want the doctors to laugh at me? I am a medic. I have been working for nine days under Israeli attack. Nothing has happened to me; do not worry about me."'

Om Yassir continued, 'He was a trainer, preparing young volunteers on first aid. He also worked as a volunteer after finishing his work at Al Shifa hospital. I was always asking him, "Isn't it enough what you do at the hospital?" He said, "Mum, they need me." There was a shortage of nurses during the war. He would go out at night-time to help people in the camp. He would say, "This man needs first aid, or this woman needs her bandage changing." He also visited some elderly people outside his work hours to check on them. He was kind, helpful. I was always so proud of him.

'He took the two briefcases and went out in the morning at 10.30 a.m. Before, he was wandering about in the house. He looked at me many times in a way I felt afterwards meant goodbye.'

She added, 'When the war started he spent four days working at Al Shifa hospital. He phoned us all the time. He cried in all his calls for the people who were savagely killed or severely injured. He told me that many people he was helping wet themselves. They were terrified. He told me in one phone call: "I am traumatized by putting so many people in the fridge in the morgue." Sadly he was put in the morgue himself. He was killed on the ninth day of the war.'

Kamal, Yassir's father, hugged his two young daughters as he continued to remember. 'We had no electricity. My wife could not bake. I went out to buy food for the family. There was a serious shortage of food in Gaza. I went everywhere. I stood in many queues, until I got some food. Moments later on Al Wilhda Street, a young man called Mohanad phoned me to inform me that Yassir was killed. I was in a state of shock. I came home; none of the family yet knew what had happened. Om Yassir was putting the washing on the line. I told her our son was martyred. She started weeping and screaming. I went to Al Shifa hospital. They gave me his belongings and told me he was in the morgue. I went to have a last look at him; he looked very peaceful.'

Om Yassir said, 'Two days before he died, he brought two tins of broad beans. He asked me if I can make "fool modammas" with olive oil. I was in a bad mood. I ignored him. On the night before he was killed, I had a very bad nightmare. I woke up and made him "fool modammas". Had I not made that dish for him, I would never have forgiven myself.

'He was married. He had a daughter called Malak. She was only 17 months old when Yassir was killed. Her mother moved to live with her family after the death of Yassir. She always brings Malak to visit us. We feel happy when Malak is with us. She reminds us of Yassir. We feel he is alive in her. We always tell her how lovely her father was. Yassir was good to his young sisters. Whatever he bought for his daughter Malak he would buy for my youngest, Amira, too. He also used to take them out for a ride on his motorcycle.

'He never stopped talking. We always teased him when he recounted a story in all its detail. I would ask him: "Do you tell the doctors at the hospital such long stories?"

'He was affiliated to Hamas but he never indulged in factional differences. He always said: "I am a nurse. I am here to do my job and to help everyone regardless of their background otherwise I should not be doing this job."

'We owe it to him that our lives were saved in 2004. Our house was completely destroyed by an Israeli Apache helicopter when they targeted the house of Abu Yousif Al Qooqa, the leader of

Salahuddin Brigades, who lived near us. [Salahuddin Brigades is one of the resistance organizations based mainly in the Gaza Strip.] They failed to kill him then but succeeded later. We were inside the house. Early in the afternoon Yassir saw people running away. He saw a helicopter hovering in the area. He rushed back to the house and told us to get out immediately. We ran out, forgetting to take my 15-day-old daughter Samar with us. After we left, we realized she was missing. My son Muhammad went back and got her out. Moments later, the Israeli Apache launched two rocket attacks. One of them destroyed our house. If it had not been for Yassir, we would all be dead by now.

'How can they attack an ambulance? How can they kill three paramedics? The lies of the Israelis make me sick, they lie about ambulances carrying weapons. It is a lie. After this incident and other attacks on ambulances, they spread fear among paramedics. Many of them were scared to go round in ambulances. For a while, civilian cars had to carry the injured to hospital.'

'I am 51 years old,' Kamal said. 'We never experienced such suffering. In my view this was the worst that we suffered. I was not alive during the 1948 Nakba. Some of the elderly in the neighbourhood who witnessed the Nakba always say that it was worse. They keep saying to me, "Think yourself lucky, yes, you lost a son but at least you are still living in the same area and have not been made a refugee. In 1948 we lost everything: loved ones, land and property." I suppose they have a point.'

Om Yassir sighed. 'It is a strange mixture of feelings I go through every day, a feeling of severe pain for the loss of Yassir but also a feeling of pride. My son died as a hero helping to save others. This is how he is remembered. He definitely left us in body but he will forever live with us through the good memory which he left among everyone who knew him, family and others. This is why I feel proud and I will continue to be.'

6

Breaking the siege

In the late afternoon I went for a walk in Gaza Port. The port is in disrepair and only a few fishing boats are scattered about the small harbour. An old, eroding platform extends into the Mediterranean. I stood there for a while watching the sea. The most important event in my life came to mind. In the afternoon of 23 August 2008 our two Free Gaza Movement rusty fishing boats, Free Gaza and Liberty, arrived here. It was an initiative which symbolically and physically broke the Israeli siege of the Gaza Strip. Thousands of Gazans, young and old, men and women, were packing the platform and the street behind the port waiting for us. None of us could believe it. Many stood in stunned silence, others were excited. Some jumped into the water and swam towards our boats. A young boy swam with one hand while carrying a Palestinian flag in the other. The crowds were waving flags and chanting our welcome in Arabic and English. We were the first two boats to enter Gaza Port since the occupation in 1967. As our boats approached many Palestinian fishing boats came out to salute us. Some of them were dangerously overloaded by people who did not care about their safety. They just wanted to greet us.

On one of the boats I saw my eldest sister Mai and her husband Mousa. Earlier she had fallen into the water in her excitement and Mousa had to jump in to rescue her. Although she can swim, restricted by her conservative religious dress she had nearly drowned. My sister Maha, her son Muhammad and bride Mariam were also waiting for us. The meeting with my sisters was incredibly emotional. We cried for a long time. People who saw me greeting my sister Mona on satellite channels thought we had not seen each other for decades, but that was not the case. We all felt a sense of freedom, combined with a strong feeling that it does not have to be this way. Why can't our family meet whenever they feel like it? I found myself hugging and kissing dozens of people – many I knew, others I did not. People around me started to sing and I joined them: 'Oh our people, you are so resilient, despite this harsh criminal siege.' I don't believe any of us could find the words to describe those moments.

Without a doubt our arrival was a breath of freedom and hope for the people of the Gaza Strip. Everyone felt a sense of pride during those euphoric moments. It was a feeling of dignity that comes from defiance when much of the world, including Arab regimes, turns a blind eye to the Palestinians' suffering. Even if we had only achieved a few moments of triumph for the people, this would have been a good enough cause for which to have campaigned.

In Gaza we were received warmly by the International and Popular Committees for Breaking the Siege and by the Hamas Government. They put us up in Al Dira, one of the most expensive hotels in the Gaza Strip. We objected because we wanted to stay with families in camps, towns or community centres so that members of the group could see for themselves the scale of suffering there. The Hamas security did not give us a choice. They were concerned about our safety and considered Al Dira to be the place where we would be best protected. The owner and staff at Al Dira were welcoming throughout our short stay. None of us had expected us to reach Gaza, so the arrangements for our four-day visit were ad hoc.

We arrived in Gaza at the height of the tension between Fateh and Hamas. Hamas had just arrested hundreds of Fateh activists, saying it was a retaliatory action for the imprisonment of hundreds of its members and leaders in the West Bank. From the first moment of our arrival we made clear we were not affiliated to any Palestinian factions. We were there for all the Palestinians regardless of their political or religious background. This was the truth. It was essential for people to know this to counter the Israeli campaign accusing us of being tools for Hamas.

On the second day of our arrival some of us sailed out with some fishermen early in the morning. We hoped the presence of internationals on the fishermen's boats would deter the Israeli navy from attacking them. It worked. The fishermen were ecstatic. They managed to catch many more tonnes of fish than usual because normally the Israelis confine them to the shallow waters.

We were invited to have dinner with the Hamas Prime Minister, Ismael Hania. He came across as a humble person. He awarded all of us the Jerusalem medal for breaking the siege. Each of us spoke for a few minutes. When our colleague Judith Lutz told him that she was Jewish, he responded through the interpreter: 'We welcome you here in Gaza: please be sure that we are not against Jews for their religious background; we are against the state of Israel for its long occupation and dispossession of our people.' In my view this was a sincerely meant statement by Hania and it would improve Hamas's political standing if other prominent leaders of the organization took the same position.

When it was my turn to speak, I thanked him and said that if he really wanted to honour members of the Free Gaza Movement, he should order the immediate release of all political prisoners in Hamas prisons. I condemned the imprisonment of Hamas members in the West Bank by the Palestinian Authority's security forces as much I condemned the imprisonment of Fateh members in Gaza. It is a blot on the leadership of both sides to imprison Palestinians because of their political affiliation.

Hania held both my hands, looked me in the eye and said he hoped that all prisoners would be released on both sides. This was not what I wanted to hear. I had hoped he would take this opportunity to make a firm commitment. Another member of the Free Gaza Movement, Therese McDermott, said, 'I support what my friend Musheir said and demand the release of all political prisoners.' Some circles in the Hamas leadership thought that I was inciting members of the Free Gaza Movement to demand the release of political prisoners. Later, my sister Mona and I repeated the same demand to the Hamas Interior Minister, the late Saeed Siyam. He told us that the Ramallah leadership had provoked them for over a year by imprisoning Hamas members in the West Bank and that they had to act to protect their members. 'Two wrongs don't make a right,' I replied. He did not promise anything specific. (Siyam was later killed by the Israelis during Operation Cast Lead.)

Our delegation went on a tour of the Beach Camp where Hania still lives. It was interesting to see his modest demeanour in dealing with his neighbours, how people received him as a neighbour rather than a Prime Minister, the way they greeted him as 'Abu El Abed' which is how one would address a friend, not a man in his political position.[12] He seemed comfortable with this. This attitude by Hamas leaders and the way they have lived among the people without any barriers or the outward trappings of authority were arguably the main reasons for their popularity and led to Hamas's landslide victory in the Palestinian Legislative Council Elections in January 2006. This image has been severely shaken, however, since Hamas seized sole power in June 2007.

We entered several houses in the camp and saw for ourselves the effect of the siege. Most households had no income. They depended on donations from the UN and non-governmental organizations. Many families we met had to sell their furniture to be able to survive. We witnessed families cooking on wooden logs because they had been forced to sell their cookers. Even those who still had a cooker found it near impossible to obtain the gas to fuel it.

On the second and third days of our stay we took most members of the delegation on a tour of the Gaza Strip from the northern border to Rafah in the south. The Free Gaza members had the chance to see for themselves the level of devastation the siege and the frequent Israeli invasions have caused. In the north we stopped at Izbit Abed Rabu. We talked to the grandfather of Iyad and Jacklene Abu Shbaak (see ch. 4, p. xx) who started to tell us the story of their killing. The old man could not finish the story and he broke down in tears. We also stopped at the Abu Holy checkpoint where thousands of Palestinians have been humiliated daily for more than five years (see ch. 16, p. 104).

---

[12] In Arab culture, a married man with children is called the father of his eldest son; in this case the eldest son of Mr Hania is called Abed, which makes him Abu El Abed.

In Khan Younis we were accompanied by the mayor, Muhammed El-Farra, and members of the council. We visited the area where pollution, a serious environmental problem, is growing by the day (see ch. 7, p. 47).

In Rafah at the south of the Gaza Strip we went to the place where the American peace activist Rachel Currie was crushed by an Israeli army Caterpillar bulldozer, while standing in full vision of the driver, in her desperate attempt to stop the demolition of a Palestinian house. We also stopped at what used to be the notorious Salahuddin Gate close to the Egyptian border. Many Palestinians were shot dead here from the military watchtower that used to overlook the whole area. It was near the Salahuddin Gate that the British peace activist Tom Hurndall was killed by an Israeli sniper in 2003. The Israeli army claimed he had been carrying a gun but it soon transpired he was helping schoolchildren cross the road when he was gunned down.

When the majority of our group departed from Gaza, some of us remained behind to accompany fishermen who face daily harassment from Israeli patrols. Their presence acted as a deterrent for a while but, a few months later, the Israeli navy attacked some Palestinian fishing boats with internationals on board. Vittorio Arrigobni, a brave and committed peace activist, was injured in one of the attacks. He needed 10 stitches to treat his injury. This did not stop him. He continued until the Israelis sprayed him with hot water and threw a net over him, arrested him together with Andrew Munice and Darlene Wallach, imprisoned and then deported them. This did not deter Vittorio who returned to Gaza through Rafah. He stayed to help Palestinian farmers and fishermen and worked hard with the medical crews to reach victims of the Israeli attacks on Gaza in the winter of 2008.

Sadly Vittorio was kidnapped by a group belonging to one of the Salafi Jihadi groups which oppose Hamas in the Gaza Strip. They demanded the release of their leader in a Hamas prison in exchange for Vittorio. The kidnappers killed Vittorio. His brutal murder was a massive shock to the Palestinians and those further afield. He was much loved by Gazans. I had got to know Vittorio during the trip to Gaza and knew he was a true internationalist. The Palestinians mourned the death of Vittorio as one of us and he will remain in the memory of most as a true fighter for justice. His motto, 'Stay human', has become a much loved slogan.

Before the Free Gaza boats left Larnaca the group agreed that since we were sailing on two boats, Free Gaza and Liberty, it would be difficult to make joint decisions. The group elected five members as a committee to decide on issues that may arise during the voyage. The three members on the Free Gaza boat were Greta Berlin, Jeff Halper and me. On Liberty the two committee members were Vangalis Passias and Paul Larudi. It was about 2.30 in the afternoon when two Israeli navy frigates, one on each side of our boats, appeared in the far distance. They followed us for three-quarters of an hour before disappearing. Shortly after, Hayan Al Jo'ba, who was with us representing the main Palestinian news agency, Ramatan, brought us the news. To our surprise, the Israeli army radio had announced that the Ministry of Foreign Affairs had decided not to obstruct the two boats. The mood changed completely. All tiredness and complaints disappeared. Even our friend, Donna Wallach, who had spent the entire journey vomiting so much that at one stage we feared for her life, became active again. We jumped up and down, hugging each other, crying and chanting.

In the middle of this jubilation we had a call on the walkie-talkie system from the Liberty boat. They suggested that since we were arriving early evening it would be better to halt and continue our voyage the following morning when the press would be there to receive us. To those of us on the Free Gaza boat this was a shock because we were all ready to continue. The dream of breaking the siege was about to come true: the press had been the last thing in our minds. These were tense moments. There were no guarantees that the Israeli cabinet would not reverse its decision overnight. We had an hour-long discussion with Liberty but it became clear we would not reach an agreement. It was put to a vote on the Committee. We had three members and they had two so we won the vote and took the decision to carry on. The group on Liberty was annoyed and when we began moving on they thought that we had abandoned them. Fortunately, after a moment, they decided to join us and we arrived in Gaza together. Once they saw the thousands waiting for us at the Gaza Port they agreed the right decision had been taken.

As Gaza started to appear on the horizon I felt ecstatic; I just could not believe it. I never expected it. After all the threats, we thought we would end up in an Israeli jail. I could not stop my tears. At last, I will be able to visit my mother Laila's grave. Laila, who always said to people around her, even when she was in good health, 'If I die, please tell him that the last words on my lips were Musheir.' My tears continued to flow.

Later, we learned from press reports that there was a dispute between the Israeli Ministry of Foreign Affairs and the Defense Ministry. The Foreign Ministry was worried we were looking for a fight in the Mediterranean to achieve a propaganda victory. The Ministry of Defense was against allowing us to reach Gaza. The Israeli Foreign Ministry's position won out. According to reports one of their officials said, 'They want to bang their heads against our wall. We will remove this wall so that they will not achieve their aim.'

As we neared the coast, Derrick, one of our colleagues, came to me asking to contact the Gaza Port authorities to seek permission to enter Gaza's territorial waters. No ships had docked in Gaza Port since 1967, so the port authorities did not know how to guide us. Derrick was adamant we should get some guidance. By then I could see Gaza clearly. I erupted in tears: 'No need, there is the Beach Camp, there is Omar Al Mukhtar Street. I can see Al Shohada Street. The port is there, right in front of us.' The celebration and tears continued. Greta Berlin hugged me and said, 'Musheir, these moments can never be taken away from us.' We had reached Gaza against all the odds.

Prior to leaving Larnaca we stayed at Nicosia, on Cyprus. All of us were under the impression that we would be sailing to Gaza within three days following our arrival there. Even our training programme was designed to reflect this short period of time. As days passed we realized no one even knew the exact date of departure. In fact, the purchase of the two boats had not been finalized. This caused a lot of frustration. The heat wave meant daily temperatures of 43 degrees Celsius. The Nicosia University accommodation, where we stayed, is built like massive concrete ships. They retain the heat and we were there at the height of summer.

David Schermerhorn piloted one of the boats in the Free Gaza flotilla. He was in his late sixties and had much maritime experience. Two days before sailing to Gaza I asked him whether our two boats would be able to make our sea voyage. With a big grin on his face David answered, 'When I saw the two boats I was shocked. I thought they were inadequate for anything more than a 20-mile fishing trip. I was worried but then I looked at all of you and said to myself: "These are a bunch of crazy guys so why wouldn't I be one?"' His reply reassured me!

In Nicosia, we got to know Nora El Shawa, a sincere and generous Palestinian woman from Gaza City who owns Al Rimal publishing company. Nora, her daughter Fadia and Cypriot friend Elli helped us enormously during the three weeks we anxiously waited to set off. Nora's presence, her warm, friendly personality and hard work behind the scenes was a source of strength at a time when I was in severe need of it. I was worrying about my two young sons Qasem and Qayis, who were 5 and 2 years old. Thinking about what could happen to them if I were hurt or even killed by the Israeli army, a real possibility, made me very upset. Nora opened her heart and home to all of us and offered help whenever any of us needed it.

The presence of Greta Berlin, a co-founder of the Free Gaza Movement, helped to calm the situation. Greta's bubbly personal-ity, her ability to absorb people's anger and her sense of humour earned our affection as the days went by without any progress on our departure date.

An interesting member of our group was Fathi Jouadi, a Tunisian cameraman and filmmaker. He is a devout Moslem, who, without compromising his principles, is a model of tolerance towards people, whatever their religion or ideology. He became one of the main pillars of the Free Gaza Movement, although it was a chance meeting that led him to us. I was a guest on a programme on Al Hiwar satellite TV in London to promote our intended Break the Siege expedition. Fathi was the cameraman. After the programme, he said to me that he liked the idea and would like to join us. In Gaza it was intriguing and heart-warming how Fathi managed to win the hearts of everyone he met. And his Tunisian Arabic accent proved popular with the locals during our stay.

The presence of Hedi Epstein, an 84-year-old Holocaust survivor, attracted media attention. As this attention grew, Hedi got fed up with it, though the rest of us welcomed it. Hedi wanted to be known as a Jewish peace activist there to help break the siege. According to Hedi true Jewish values emphasized helping your neighbours, not uprooting them and committing atrocities against them. Sadly, Hedi fell ill three days before our departure. The doctors advised her not to sail and she had to stay behind.

We discussed what we would do if one of us died on board. Greta, in her strong commitment to reach Gaza, no matter what, got carried away, 'We are sailors. We will wrap him or her in a flag, give them the deserved respect and salute and toss them overboard.' Greta said this very seriously. I will never forget the shocked look on Cathleen O'Connor's face who was sitting next to Greta. 'We cannot do that,' Cathleen said. Greta realized what she had just said and laughed loudly, 'Oh yes, I forgot we will not be sailing for six months.' We all agreed we should go back to Larnaca if a death occurred. We laughed a lot over Greta's old sea dog attitude.

The Free Gaza experience had not been without internal problems: it is difficult to reach decisions between people who share the same goal but have different approaches. The first disagreement occurred when some members of the group suggested that with three Israeli friends among us, the Israeli flag should be hoisted on the boat along with the flags representing the nationalities of the other activists. Comrades who suggested this did not intend any offence but they failed to appreciate the flag's significance for Palestinians, for whom the Israeli flag represents more than six decades of oppression and violence. Every Israeli weapon of aggression; every military tower that watches over us and kills our people; every jet fighter that bombs our homes; every bulldozer which uproots our trees and destroys our land and houses; every checkpoint that humiliates us; and every prison that holds our political prisoners is symbolized by that flag. To have raised it on a mission breaking the siege of Gaza would have been to ignore their sense of injustice. Our three Israeli friends, Jeff Helper, Donna and Darlene Wallach did not object. The first problem was resolved.

The second point of difference was over how we should define our initiative to try to break the siege. Was it humanitarian or political? Again, we had long discussions. We agreed that its aim was to defend human rights but it was also political. The whole idea behind breaking the siege was to challenge the illegitimate Israeli siege of the Gaza Strip and highlight Israel's claim to have international law on its side in imposing a siege on a neighbouring area for security reasons. This amounts to the collective punishment of 1.5 million people and is, therefore, a war crime under international law. Of course, there was an element of humanitarian assistance to the mission but it was definitely not our primary aim. What we could take with us on the two small fishing boats would not be enough for more than a handful of people.

We also spent long hours discussing whether we should give permission to the Israeli navy to inspect our two boats. A group of us thought that we should. By doing this we could prove that we had nothing to hide and demonstrate to the world that we do not intend to cause trouble. Another group, including me, thought that giving permission to the Israeli navy to inspect would imply that we accept its legitimacy in the international water off the Gaza Strip. Moreover, we would not be able to stop them inspecting if they wanted to, so why give them permission? None of us had any intention to resist violently and after much discussion we agreed we would not grant them permission to inspect.

We decided to make our own banners to display on the two boats. Some thought the slogan 'Free Palestine' should not be used because it could imply our desire to destroy the state of Israel and therefore upset Israelis. Following some debate we decided to use the slogan 'Free Palestine'.

These discussions reflected a type of politics which I term 'wishy-washy'. In my view, many pro-Palestinian activists are too concerned about how the Israeli people will feel about anti-Israeli campaigns. Israel as it stands qualifies, away from rhetoric, for the status of a criminal state. This is true due to its never-ending war crimes against the Palestinians, starting with the ethnic cleansing in 1948 until the present. When this understanding is reached among all pro-Palestinian activists, then the different campaigns will move forward with more strength.

Israeli propaganda tried to intimidate us into stopping our mission. An article entitled 'the Hate Ship' was published in the Israeli newspaper *Ma'ariv* on 5 August 2008. It accused us of being apologists for one of the most sinister and fanatical regimes in the world (Hamas), members of a satanic cult and hypocrites, who are in no position to preach to anybody about peace and human rights. The article attacked our friend, Hedy Epstein, describing her as a token Jew. Her family perished in the Holocaust. She herself left Germany in 1939. It was alleged she was saved from the gas chamber but now supported a regime which kills its own people by means of gas.

The intimidation continued. We received a letter before departure from Naom Katz, one of the directors of the Israeli Ministry of Foreign Affairs. He stated the Israeli government is willing to ensure that all our humanitarian aid would be delivered to Gaza. He claimed that by doing this our mission's aim would be accomplished and we would not need to sail to the Gaza Strip. We wrote back to explain that we aimed to break the illegitimate and inhuman siege of Gaza. His reply was threatening, claiming that by rejecting the Israeli offer to deliver the aid material we had proven we were a terrorist group intent on helping a terrorist regime. 'You will be treated accordingly,' he told us.

There followed other threats. The most worrying was a phone call to Lauren Booth's family in France. An anonymous caller phoned her daughter and told her that her mother would be blown up while out on the sea. Greta Berlin received another phone call. The caller said sarcastically, 'I hope that you are able to swim because you will need it.' Several of us received similar phone calls.

A group of us, Fathi Jouadi, Andrew Munice, Eliza Earnshire, Maria Delmar, Adam Qvist and I were sitting outside one of the halls of residence making banners. At 2.30 a.m. we noticed three people walking through the building. We first thought they were students. When they stopped on the second floor, watching us, we started to get concerned. When we shouted asking what they wanted, they disappeared. We followed them. They went into a different section of the building and when they saw us they started to run towards the car park. We called the security guard and caught up with them. They were visibly nervous. They claimed they were on their way back from Larnaca when they noticed the student accommodation and since they were architects, they stopped to have a look. Their story did not stack up. The student accommodation is not visible from the Larnaca to Nicosia road, especially after midnight. We asked the security guard to stop them or take their details but to our disappointment, he did not want to follow it up and let them leave. From then on we guarded our accommodation at night, in shifts, until we left.

The most worrying threat came 36 hours before leaving Larnaca for Gaza. The Cypriot port authorities informed us they had received an Israeli navy communiqué declaring the international waters facing the Gaza Strip to be a military zone from 22 August 2008. That date was the day before our intended departure. The communiqué stated Israel would be carrying out military exercizes, including the planting of sea mines. They warned any vessels against entering this area. This was serious.

We held a meeting in Larnaca and I said that, in view of the threat, I would understand, as a Palestinian, if people decided to withdraw. The first response came from Sister Ann Montgomery, a nun in her eighties, 'When I decided to join the Free Gaza Movement I was not thinking of myself, but of the suffering of the people of Gaza. This threat will not change my mind. I will carry on.' Then came other responses. No one was intimidated. On the contrary, this threat made us more fired up to go.

On the night before our departure, some of us slept on board the fishing boats to protect them from any attempt at sabotage by the Israeli navy SEALs. In 1988 they had bombed the engines of the Return Ship which had been due to sail from Larnaca to Palestine with more than two hundred Palestinian refugees on board. We feared the same happening again. We thought with some of us on board the Israelis may think twice before blowing the boats up for

Noor at Gaza Beach, summer 2008

Asil and Noor

The Deeb family sitting in the yard outside the house, Samir on the right.

Muhammad Mounir in a wedding party

Muhammad Mu'in at the front of the house

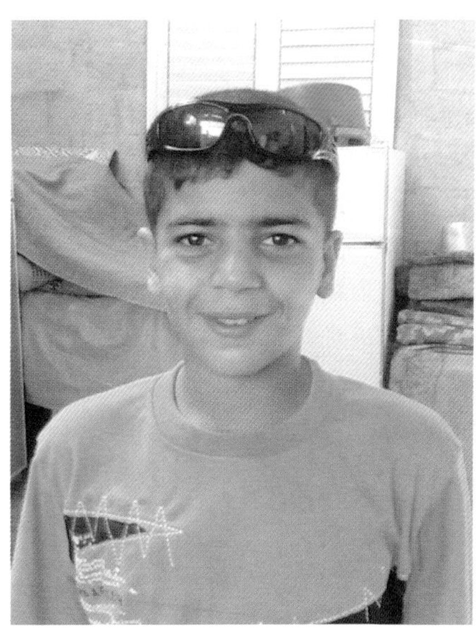

Isam Samir Deeb

Hajja Shammah with one of
her grandchildren

The dough Ayah and Fatima
were preparing

Mu'in with the bodies of three of his children

The front yard after the massacre

Tahani with the photo of
Mustafa

Sufian and Ghassan on their
wedding day

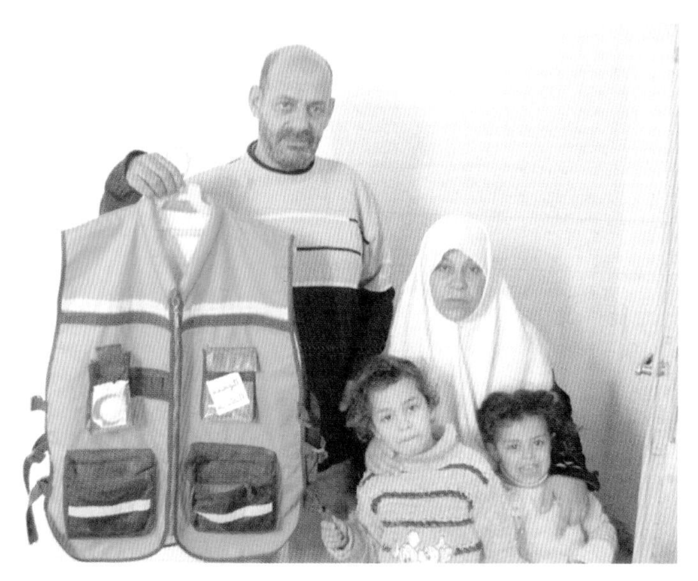

Yassir's parents and sisters with the jacket he was wearing when he was killed

Gaza is appearing, we are trying to estabalish contact

Minutes before arriving at
Gaza Port

Thousands in Gaza Port welcoming
the boats

Vittorio Arragoni with the author on the right

Carlos Latuff, Brazilian cartoonist (© Carlos Latuff, used with permission)

fear of an international outcry. It worked. Just before we left a group of Cypriot navy divers inspected the bottom of the two boats to make sure no sabotage had taken place.

A few days before our departure we held a ceremony to remember the 14 Palestinian fishermen who have been killed by the Israeli navy since 2000. The ceremony was also in remembrance of the 34 American marines who were killed when the Israeli air force attacked and destroyed the USS Liberty, an enormous spy ship loaded with the latest eavesdropping gear.[13] As Sister Ann

---

[13] Bamford writes:

Three days after Israel had launched the 1967 six-day war, Egyptian prisoners of war in the Sinai had become a burden for their captors. There was another way to deal with them.

As the Liberty sat within sight of El Arish (a town in the Sinai desert, 80 kilometres south of Gaza city), to eavesdrop on surrounding communications, Israeli soldiers turned the town into a slaughterhouse. An eyewitness recounted how in the shadow of the El Arish mosque, they lined up about 60 unarmed Egyptian prisoners, hands tied behind their backs, and then opened fire until the pale desert sand turned red.

This and other war crimes Israel had sought to conceal since the start of the conflict. They lied about the Egyptian threat, lied about who started the war, lied to the UN Security Council, lied to the press, lied to the public.

The aerial and naval attack left 34 US marines dead and two-thirds of the rest of the crew wounded. Israel asked President Johnson to bury the incident. A total news ban was ordered by the Pentagon.

President Lyndon Johnson commented that he didn't care if the ship had been sunk, he would not embarrass his allies. An Israeli court of inquiry completely exonerated the government and all those involved. No one was ever court-martialled. On the contrary, Israel chose instead to honour the motor torpedo boat, which had fired at the Liberty.

Despite the overwhelming evidence that Israel had attacked the ship deliberately, the Johnson administration covered up the entire incident. Johnson was planning to run for president the following year and needed the support of pro-Israel voters. (James Bamford, *Body of Secrets* (London: Century, 2001). Extracted in *The Guardian*, 8 August 2001.)

Montgomery and I read the names of the American marines and the Palestinian fishermen, Mary Hughes and Huwaida Araf, a Palestinian from inside the Green Line and one of the coordinators of the Free Gaza Movement, threw a rose into the sea for each of the victims.

The families of the Liberty victims are still trying to get the American administration to reveal the facts about what happened to their sons. Some of them contacted the Free Gaza Movement and asked that one of our boats be called Liberty in remembrance of their dead sons. We agreed unanimously.

My participation in Free Gaza's, Break the Siege expedition was triggered by two factors. Firstly, I cannot just stand by and watch while a war crime in the form of the imprisonment of 1.5 million people is taking place.

The second was very personal. I was born in Gaza, in Khan Younis. It is the place of my childhood memories: my first nursery, school, childhood friends, shops where I bought sweets, people I love very much. Yet I am denied the freedom to go there.

On 11 July 2007 the phone rang. It was my eldest brother Manar, who lives in Jordan, at the other end: 'I have bad news Musheir,' he said. 'Mama has been taken to Nassir hospital in Khan Younis with internal bleeding. Try your best to go back as it is impossible for me with a Palestinian passport to be allowed to enter the Gaza Strip. You stand a better chance with your British passport.' My sister Mona was visiting her kids who study in Manchester. She was stuck there because of the siege. We both rushed to get permission from the Israeli authorities to enter. The British Consulate in Jerusalem failed to get us the permission. They kept repeating that the Israeli authorities will deny us permission. 'We have no power. We just ask them.' Their attitude was not what one would expect from an embassy representing the rights of its citizens. This is a deeply felt grievance by many Palestinians who hold British citizenship and have asked for help in the past.

Mona tried through her contacts in the UN. We also applied for permission through an Israeli human rights organization, Physicians for Human Rights Israel (PHRI). Mona had previously dealt with them over trying to get Palestinian patients permission to leave the Gaza Strip for medical treatment after they had been refused. Ron from the PHRI sympathized with us and tried his best to help.

For nine long days we kept trying, to no avail. During this time, I phoned the hospital several times a day. My mother was dying. The doctors confirmed that there was no hope of recovery. She was drifting in and out of a coma but I managed to speak to her a few times. Her speech was slurred and she kept repeating the names of her children. Only one sister, Maha, managed to be at her bedside. Manar could not get back from Jordan and neither could my brother Mones, who was in Egypt or my eldest sister Mai, who was visiting her children in the USA. All we wanted was to visit our dying mother in the hospital where all of us were born: what people in other countries take for granted. I kept saying to my mother that I would soon be at her bedside. It was a pledge I was unable fulfil. On 19 July, nine days after my mother's admission to hospital, I received a phone call at 4.45 a.m. from Muhand, a young neighbour who was very close to my mother. *Your mother has passed away*. I did not wake up my family. I went downstairs, picked up a photo of my mother, hugged it and cried at the loss of the person dearest to my heart.

I used to joke with my mother, 'Do not die when I cannot be with you.' She would laugh and say, 'Don't worry, I will not if you promise to place me in my grave with your own hands.' I had promised to do it but was unable to. Five hours after the death of my mother, we were informed that the PHRI managed to obtain a verbal permission for my sister Mona and I to go back.

On the morning the Break the Siege boats were due to depart from Gaza Port, I woke up early. I went to the Khan Younis cemetery with Fathi Jouadi to visit my mother's grave. It was the first time I had visited the grave. I spontaneously found myself talking to my mother. I could not stop my tears. I kept saying, 'Mother, I am here. I am visiting you despite their siege.' It was a wonderful feeling of freedom I had never experienced on any previous visits. It was the first time in my life I had visited home without the humiliation of being questioned or interrogated by the Israelis, threatened, having my travel documents thrown in my face, and without knowing whether I would be able to get in or not. It is a sense of liberation I hope every Palestinian will experience one day. I am proud of being the first Palestinian from the Occupied Territories to enter Palestine without Israeli permission since 1967.

My mother's origins were in the Caucuses, from an ethnic group called the Circassians. Her grandparents escaped with their families along with tens of thousands of others from the brutality of the Russian Tsars at the turn of the last century. The Tsar gave them the choice of converting from Islam to Russian Orthodox Christianity or being massacred. Some converted, others, including my grandfather's family, fled their towns and villages to Jordan where my mother was born. When she was 1 year old my grandparents divorced. My grandmother Om Hamida moved from Jordan to live in Palestine, the place my mother loved and belonged to more than anywhere on earth. They lived in Haifa when my mother was little, then Tubas, Nablus, Tulkarim, Ramallah and finally Khan Younis. There she worked as a teacher and, then headmistress, for several decades at a school at Ma'an in the south of Khan Younis.

The story of my mother and father getting married is interesting. My father Qasem was a proud man who always dressed elegantly in modern suits. This was almost unique in Khan Younis in the 1940s. My mother as a stranger to the area also dressed differently from the locals. She wore a dress suit with a hat. She was the only woman in Khan Younis who dressed this way. In a small town like Khan Younis it was inevitable that they would notice each other and eventually my father asked to marry her. My grandmother agreed after making enquiries. The main problem was my grandfather in Jordan, who was furious about the whole thing. To him a Circassian woman had to marry a Circassian man. He came all the way from Jordan with a group of Circassian notables to try to stop the marriage. However, my grandmother stood her ground and won the argument. For a woman to have her way in the 1940s was an impressive achievement.

Etched in my memory from childhood is my mother crying as she told us of the Palestinian struggle in the thirties. She told tales of revolutionaries and martyrs, of the tears always shed for loved ones that were killed, and of the injustice that still prevails. I remember listening and crying with her.

I will never forget an autumn night in the seventies. I was 11 years old when a large group of Israeli soldiers stormed our house, as they did frequently in occupied Palestine. My mother was fierce when defending us. On that evening my mother kept cursing all Arab leaders who claim day and night that they are the protectors of defenceless Palestinians, yet do nothing to help.

Zakaria, one of my mother's pupils, told me once, 'I am indebted to your mother in two big ways: for teaching and disciplining me for six years and secondly because of an incident in 1972 when I was 9 years old. After throwing stones at an Israeli army jeep, I ran through Ma'an school yard. The soldiers got off their jeep and followed me. Your mother came out of her office to stop them as she always did by closing the school's main gate. When the soldiers kept pushing, she pushed back with the help of some teachers. She shouted: "This is an educational institution, you have no right to enter." Eventually, the soldiers pushed their way thorough and she fell to the ground. But by that time, I was on the far side of the school's concrete wall, disappearing into the adjacent fields.'

I was deeply touched by Zakaria's story.

In 1975 the Israeli military governor of the Gaza Strip held a meeting with the UN education officials and all headteachers from UN schools. 'Teach your pupils that their homeland is where they were born not where their parents or grandparents were born,' the military governor told them. This was clearly aimed at teaching children to forget their right of return to their homes in pre-1948 Palestine. Laila interrupted him: 'I am an educator,' she said. 'I cannot lie: their homeland is Asdod, Yafa, Al Majdal, Bir Al Saba'a and other areas inside the Green Line. How about you: you were born in Poland. Why don't you practise what you preach? Why did you come to Palestine to uproot its indigenous population?' The Israeli military governor furiously banged his hand on the table and declared the meeting finished. He complained strongly to the UN. The director of the UN education authority in the Gaza Strip, Badi' Quffah, carried out an investigation. In the end he did not take any action. Such was Laila, she would speak the truth, and fear no one.

Laila's contribution to the field of education in Khan Younis is still recognized by everyone in the area. Her pupils affectionately refer to her as 'Mistress'. Many of them went onto higher education. She was proud of them and had a close relationship with the people in Ma'an area. She compared her office to a tribal Chief's headquarters, from where over three decades she dispensed advice to resolve domestic problems. My mother's motto will live with me forever: 'If a nation has lost its moral values, it ceases to exist.'

The death of my mother with me unable to do the normal things – to sit at her bedside during her last moments, to receive the final kiss of farewell – will remain a source of pain for me forever.

7

Paradise polluted

My flashback ended and to return to Khan Yhounis, I chose to take the beach road linking Gaza to the middle part of the Gaza Strip, to enjoy the beauty of the sunset on Gaza beach after what had been another traumatic day. I was looking for a brief respite from the horrific stories I was hearing. A friend of mine once told me that there is only one way to escape the tragedy of the Gaza Strip: sit on the beach and look west, towards the sea, with your back to the Gaza Strip. I guess that she was right in the physical sense. There are many lovely things in Gaza but they are to do with the good nature of the people rather than the current physical environment.

The beach road is slightly above sea level. At some stage just before the turning into Nussirat refugee camp, the road dips down for a short distance and then rises again. This landmark is known to the Gazans as *Wadi Gaza*, the Gaza Valley, which is the only nature reserve in the Gaza Strip. The valley area reaches across central Gaza, from east to the west, continuing uninterrupted towards the Mediterranean. This *wadi* extends from southern Hebron in the West Bank, a place called *Wadi Khalil*, near Alsamou Village, to the Gaza Strip, running about 15 kilometres into the Naqab (Negev) desert. The *wadi* is the only place where sea birds can be seen.

The Gaza Valley has become a sewage and rubbish dump for residents of Gaza and Israel, the occupying power. Israeli warplanes and tanks ceaselessly shell the area with missiles and rockets. The ground is now a toxic dump, depleted with lethal chemical wastes, such as lead and uranium: hazardous not only to the environment, but also to the residents living in the area.

The valley is a proposed nature reserve, but larger mammals and birds are nearly extinct, as are the flowers and the trees. The clean ground water has almost vanished.

The smell of sewage is very strong. It is no exaggeration to say that it is unbearable to spend more than a few minutes there. This was December when the toxic smell is expected to decrease due to the cold weather. I did not want to think about what it would be like in summer. It was never like that when I was a child. It was at the top of that road's incline, close to the junction with the Nussairat refugee camp, where my parents used to take us to the famous Al Nowairy cafe/restaurant. It is one of the most stunning spots on the Gaza Strip beaches. It used to be a special place where many Gazans loved to go to for the delicious charcoal grilled chicken and the fantastic selection of salads. Its simple yet charming atmosphere made this restaurant special. It is similar to any *Areesha*; Gazans build these on top of their houses in heavily populated areas to avoid the summer heat. It is a structure made of metal pipes and covered with palm fronds. Unfortunately, the place has changed as a result of long years of Israeli occupation and siege. It has stopped serving food: it survives by serving tea, coffee and hubbly bubbly (a water pipe).

Momentarily, I travelled back in time to when I was a child in the early 1970s. I always wanted to be good, hoping my parents would fulfil their promise and take me with my brother Mones to Al Nowairy. It made me sad to think that such a lovely spot has turned into a heavily polluted area. We would order the food and, while it was being prepared, Mones and I would swim in the sea. The owner was a friend of my father. It was interesting that when it came to paying the bill, a friendly argument in typical Gazan style would take place. My father would try to pay and Al Nowairy would refuse. 'Come on, it is your livelihood; you can invite me to your house, not here.' 'No way will I take the money,' Al Nowairy would answer. My father would then leave the money on the table and depart. Despite everything people in the Gaza Strip have suffered over long decades of war, oppression and poverty, they are genuinely warm and generous.

The colour of the sea has changed; it is no longer crystal clear as it used to be. I had mixed feelings. I was shocked, but I also had a sense of my naivety. What did I expect after all these years of Israeli occupation and policies that systematically destroy the Palestinian environment? The siege of the Gaza Strip has exposed these policies. Swimming in the Mediterranean around the Gaza Strip has become a serious hazard in recent years. Thousands of families still visit the beaches every summer without realizing the scale of the pollution.

According to the UN Office for the Coordination of Humanitarian Affairs (OCHA) 50 to 60 million litres of untreated and partially treated sewage was poured into the sea surrounding the Gaza Strip every day in 2008. The amount is always on the increase. One of their reports in 2008 stated: 'This sewage cannot be treated due to the lack of a steady electricity supply in the Gaza Strip.' The OCHA has expressed concern the sea is becoming dirt-ier and more contaminated because of the chronic shortages of fuel and spare parts. 'Gaza's sewage treatment plants urgently need fourteen days of uninterrupted power in order to run a proper sewage treatment cycle, for the sake of Gaza's public health.' This is something that the Gaza Strip has not been able to achieve for more than four years. Israel is severely restricting the entry of essential spare parts for Gaza's sewage and waste water treatment plants. None of the sewage treatment plants are functioning normally. At some beaches, bathers are now, literally, swimming in sewage according to the OCHA and the Palestinian Centre for Human Rights (PCHR) in its October 2008 report.

For the same reasons unfiltered tap water is saline and undrinkable throughout the Gaza Strip given its high nitrate and chloride levels – six to seven times higher than the World Health Organization (WHO) safe levels. The WHO recently took samples from 30 Gaza Strip seashore sites, and tested them for human and animal fecal contaminants. Thirteen areas, covering seven beaches along the Gaza Strip, were identified as polluted and unsuitable for swimming, including three beaches along the central and southern Gaza Strip and four beaches in and around Gaza City, including the beach next to Gaza harbour. There is now widespread concern about the state of the Mediterranean. Gaza's sanitation services are being stretched to breaking point. It is obvious that access to clean water should be a basic human right. For Gazans the sea is an integral part of their lives; to fish, swim, eat Qidra (one of the most famous foods in Gazan cuisine – a rice- and red-meat-based food cooked with much garlic and spices in a clay pot in the oven), have a barbeque or play in the sun on the beach on a summer's day was part of daily life.

Along the beach road, I arrived at north-west Khan Younis, the second largest city in the Gaza Strip after Gaza. Khan Younis is home to 400,000 people with no sewage system. There have been many attempts by donor countries, mainly Japan, to finance the construction of a sewage system for the city and its neighbouring towns and villages. All past attempts have come to nothing because Israel intervened. On one occasion, a sewage treatment plant was to be constructed on land near the Jewish settlement, Navi Dakalim, close to Khan Younis beach. The municipality had planned a ceremony to inaugurate the start of the project. The mayor was there, notables of the city, representatives from the Japanese government and members of the public. As the ceremony started a small number of heavily armed Israeli settlers stormed the place firing in the air and chased everyone off the site. They issued a threat that anyone approaching this land would be shot on the spot. The project was abandoned.

Following the Oslo Agreement and the establishment of the Palestinian Authority another project was started and nearly completed. Only a further 1.8 kilometres of concrete pipeline was needed to reach the proposed sewage discharge site but Israel would not allow the remaining pipes to be put in place. As a result, the project had to be abandoned, leading to a serious environmental problem which is escalating by the day. As a temporary measure, the municipality of Khan Younis had to excavate more than 400 dunums (a dunum is a thousand square metres) of agricultural land to create the first sewage lake on the north-west side of the city. It was filled within weeks; they then built a second and a third and so on. The agricultural land is being gradually transformed into contaminated land.

8

A chip on my shoulder

I arrived back at my family's house in Khan Younis physically and emotionally exhausted to find relatives there. There is no chance to rest when you come home after a long time abroad. Friends and family are always visiting to welcome you; a sweet yet tiring part of Palestinian culture.

Being from Khan Younis has given me a chip on my shoulder: I share the frustration of all in the town about the lack of knowledge both in the West and the Arab world of what we all know as the 1956 Khan Younis massacre. The truth about the people whom I and everyone in my neighborhood knew was twisted into falsehood. In the Israeli version Palestinian *fedayeen* (guerrillas) were killed when Israeli forces were still facing armed resistance. The full details of the Khan Younis massacre cannot be recounted without taking a massive part of this book. In brief: during the short Israeli invasion of Sinai and the Gaza Strip which started on 29 October 1956, the town of Khan Younis and the adjacent UN refugee camp were occupied by Israeli troops on the morning of 3 November. The Israeli army committed a massacre in Khan Younis, killing a large number of Palestinian men, women and children. The massacre occurred while the camp was still under curfew.

The Israeli army lined hundreds of civilians against the walls and executed a great number in cold blood. Residents of the town and camp insist all resistance had ceased at the time of the massacre and that many unarmed civilians were killed as the Israeli troops went through the town and camp.

> Henry Labouisse, the American director of UNRWA, has received from sources he considers trustworthy lists of names of persons killed . . . [including] UNRWA employees, both refugees and others, on 3 November, numbering 275 individuals, of whom 140 were refugees and 135 local residents of Khan Younis. There was another massacre, at the Rafah refugee camp in the same area 9 days later, with 111 reported killed. The source for information on the victims at Rafah is the same.

General Burns, commander of the UN Truce Supervision forces, said that this gave 'very sad proof of the fact that the spirit that inspired the notorious Deir Yassin massacre of 1948 is not dead among some of the Israeli armed forces.'[14] I also saw corroboratory reports by the head of the Gaza observer force, Lt.-Col. R.F. Bayard of the US army, and by the editor of the Israeli newspaper, *Al Hamishmar*, Mark Gefen, who was an eyewitness to atrocities including wanton killing, for example, the murder of a doctor at Gaza hospital by an Israeli soldier. At Khan Younis, Gefen was 'shocked' to see 'bloody bodies on the ground, smashed heads . . . no one bothered to remove them . . . I was still unaccustomed to the sight of a "human" slaughter house . . .' He reports that atrocities continued until the then Israeli Prime Minister, Ben-Gurion, himself gave orders to stop the looting, murder and robbery.

I was very young, six or seven years old, when I started to hear the stories about what happened. It was not in a news report or any other form of media coverage. It was told to me by my mother

[14] On 9 April 1948, in Deir Yassin village outside Jerusalem, the Irgun and Lehi Zionist paramilitary militias, headed by Menachem Begin (who became the Israeli Prime Minister in 1977), killed 107 Palestinian civilians, half of them women and children, according to Beir Zeit University Centre for Research and Documentation of Palestinian Society in the West Bank; the number is quoted as 250 in other sources. Stories of the massacre spread terror among Palestinian villagers all over: especially after the Zionist militias paraded the terrified survivors on the back of a lorry in Jerusalem, then dumped them in the eastern part of the city. The Deir Yassin massacre was a pivotal part of the uprooting of the Palestinians.

Laila, my late aunties Alia and Ruqaiya, our beloved neighbour, Om Siham Wadi, and many others. I only need to walk no further than a few dozen metres in any direction from our Khan Younis house to come across a home which lost loved ones, either on the walls of Khan Younis castle, or inside their own houses.

My mother's good friend, Auntie Madiha Al Batta, lost two of her brothers (Hassan and Nadid) in the massacre. They were shot dead inside their house despite pleas from the horrified family. Hassan was married, with two young children, Hani and Rabab.

Another friend of my late mother was Fatima Omara, or Auntie Om Muhammad, as we used to call her. She was a very gentle woman who was full of love for everyone in the neighbourhood and beyond. She was married to Abdul Hamid Taqash, a teacher and a poet who was in his late twenties in 1956. The family fled their town Isdud inside the Green Line following attacks by the Zionist militias in 1948.[15] Their eldest daughter Fadwa, although only 6 years old, remembered the horrific scenes which took place in their house: 'We fled our house in the town to my grandmother's in Khan Younis camp after we heard about the killing that was taking place in the town,' Fadwa recounted. 'The following day, my father thought that it was safer to go back to our rented house in the town as it had a concrete roof. A few hours after we arrived, the Israeli soldiers stormed our house; they actually broke the main door. Minutes earlier, my uncle Abdullah was trying to comfort us children. He kept throwing me in the air and catching me. The soldiers lined up my father, Uncle Abdullah (22) and Uncle Yassin (14) in front of the palm tree in the front yard. They shot Uncle Abdullah in the heart: he died instantaneously. Then they shot Uncle Yassin in the legs many times.

---

[15] Isdud village is located 35 kilometres north-east of Gaza. It was mostly destroyed by Zionist militias in Operations Yo'av and ha-Har following its occupation on 28 October 1948, with the exception of its two schools, its crumbling mosque, and one of its shrines. Isdud's inhabitants were completely ethnically cleansed. The population of Asdod was 4,910 (290 Jewish) in 1945. (www.Palestineremembered.com)

'I got hysterical: I ran towards my father and clung on to his shirt braces. They started shooting at him: 14 bullets went through his back and right hand. Miraculously I was not injured. My father kept bleeding for three days. The family could not take him to hospital because of the strict curfew. My mother was seven months pregnant; she was not well but tried everything to stop the bleeding. She used coffee and cotton to press on the wounded parts. On the fourth day the curfew was lifted. My father was taken to the Baptist hospital in Gaza. His wounds were very severe; especially in the right hand. Doctors had to amputate it.

'We did not have anything to carry the body of Uncle Abdullah on. My Auntie Khadija, with the help of neighbours, took the bathroom door off its frame to take the body to the cemetery. They were very painful moments for everyone as my uncle was such a lovely man. He was looking forward to the future after finishing his apprenticeship at a UN centre in different fields.

'My father came home from hospital but his injury was still in need of daily attention there. To add insult to injury the Israeli army stormed our house again and arrested him. They accused him of writing anti-Israeli occupation graffiti on the walls: very ridiculous and false accusations as my father was firstly very ill; he was also right-handed. My mother took me every day with my sister Najwa and brother Muhammad to wait outside Nassir hospital in Khan Younis for the prison car carrying my father to hospital. We would wave at him and he would smile back at us.

'My mother gave birth to a baby boy in January 1957. My parents decided to call him Abdullah after my late uncle. One of the most painful moments for my father was when he could not hug baby Abdullah properly for the first time as he had only one hand.

Fadwa was outraged when I told her that the Israelis are denying carrying out any massacre in Khan Younis in 1956, claiming that all the people who were killed were *fedayeen*. 'We are used to their never-ending lies: however, I do not think they will be able to hide the truth any longer about the crimes they committed and are committing; not only in Khan Younis but all over Palestine.'

I left Fadwa to meet a good friend I had not seen for years. Jawdat, currently working as a doctor in Khan Younis, is the son of a respectable civil servant, 33-year-old Majdi Barbakh, who was killed on the walls of the castle.

Jawdat was 6 years old when the shelling by the Israeli army intensified on Khan Younis town. 'My pregnant mother Om Faisal fled the house fearing for our lives. She took me, my 9-year-old brother Faisal and 3-year-old sister Fatima to stay with one of our relatives who lived in Khan Younis camp. She thought it was safer there. My father was hiding in an underground shelter belonging to a neighbour alongside dozens of other civilians. At night, when the shelling stopped temporarily, my father insisted on going back to our house. Many relatives came to hide with us.

'The following morning the soldiers occupied the minaret of the Sunni mosque we could see from our house. One of my relatives carried me on his shoulder: he took off his white headscarf and asked me to wave it at the soldiers as a sign of surrender. Minutes later the soldiers stormed our house. They asked what all these people were doing there. My father explained their shelter was overcrowded so they had come to stay with us until they could get home. My father said he worked for the local municipality – he showed his work ID but the soldiers would not listen. They violently forced them out, took them to the town square. They were lined up on the castle wall. Saeed Al Najar, one of the survivors, told me that my father said just minutes before he was killed, "This is the end; let's say our prayers." Then the soldiers opened fire: my father was killed together with my uncles Atta and Yousif and many others. I will never forget as long as I live the image of my mother, grandmother and my aunties screaming hysterically when they were told what had happened.

'When I grew older I started to play table tennis at the local sports centre which was established by the UN. I became friends with one of the players, Nasooh Al Sadoony. What was impressive about Nasooh is that he was a good player despite the amputation of his right leg above the knee. I knew that Nasooh lost his right leg in 1956 Massacre. However, it was shocking to hear the details of what happened to him and his family, as he has been told it by his parents. "I was 18 months old in 1956 when the Israeli soldiers entered Block B in Khan Younis camp where our house was. The extended family was inside. They ordered my four uncles to get out and lined them up on the external wall. They first shot my 35-year-old Uncle Ibrahim who was married with one son and two daughters. Then they shot my 20-year-old uncle who had just got married one week earlier. I was terrified as everyone in the house was screaming hysterically. I got out of the house and ran towards my uncles: my 30-year-old Uncle Sobhi (who was married with one son and one daughter) carried me, trying to protect me. He shouted, 'I beg you soldier; for the sake of this little baby.' The soldiers shot both of us. I was injured in my right leg. Uncle Khamis survived and the rest of the family fled the house. My three injured uncles continued to bleed from the morning until sunset: then they died one after the other. I continued to bleed until the following morning. No one dared to move us anywhere as the Israeli soldiers were killing everyone who moved in the streets of Khan Younis and the camp. The following morning, after the declaration of the ceasefire, some passersby took me to the Baptist hospital in Gaza City. The wound was gangrenous and the doctors decided to amputate my right leg. The strange part of my story is that my family did not know my whereabouts for three months: they were ecstatic when they found out that I was still alive."'

Jamal Shublaq has been a good friend of mine since childhood. When I mentioned to him I was writing a chapter about the 1956 Khan Younis massacre, he told me two of his uncles and two cousins were among the victims. I was embarrassed as I did not know anything about it.

We went together to see one of his cousins, Salah Shublaq (74), a survivor, who told us what happened on that horrific day. 'I was a member of the *fedayeen* resistance group based in the east of Khan Younis. When I heard about the massacre being committed by the Israeli army I got very worried. I rushed back to my family house; I did not find any of them there. I found out that my parents decided to flee our house when they heard of the ongoing killing in the town. They went to my Uncle Hamouda's house which is further from the town square where the killing was taking place. Many members of our family were also hiding there; I managed to join them. At approximately sunset, my cousin Kamel went out to try to find food for us all. He was arrested by the Israeli soldiers, taken to the castle wall and executed alongside a large number of other men. When the rest of the family heard of Kamel's killing, they were terrified.'

Jamal, who was not born then, remembered what his father, Hashim, told him. When Hashim asked them all to leave to go to one of their relatives in Khan Younis camp they refused. They believed the Israeli army was only looking for *fedayeen* and since they were all civilians except for Salah (who threw his gun away at the request of the family) no harm could come to them. 'My father was very angry and left for the camp; that is how he survived,' Jamal said.

Salah continued, 'An hour later, a group of Israeli soldiers stormed the house, lined me, my brother Tala'at, cousins Muhammad and Mahmoud up on one of the walls and opened fire in front of my parents and relatives. The three of them died. I was injured severely. They thought all of us were dead so they left. Following the ceasefire the following day, my father, with the help of two elderly neighbours, started to move the bodies to Khan Younis cemetery. They could not move me to hospital until the Red Cross helped. I was transferred to the Baptist hospital in Gaza as I was bleeding heavily.'

Luckily for my own family, my parents, Qasem and Laila, were in Egypt at the time of the 1956 war. This was a great relief as some locals stated that my father's name was on the hitlist of the invading Israeli army. My grandmother Fatima (Om Hamida) took my brothers, Manar (13) and Muneir (6), and my sisters, Mai (11), Maha (9) and Mona (2), to stay with a good friend of the family, Uncle Kamal El Bournu, who lived to the west of Khan Younis. He was the head of the agricultural directorate in the area. My grandmother thought it would be safer there.

The house had a large cellar in which dozens of terrified locals were seeking refuge. They were all crammed in. My grandmother got so fed up: she could not take the crowded atmosphere any more. She said to my brothers and sisters, 'There is a God down here in the cellar and the same God is upstairs.' Manar, Mai and Maha remember the next events clearly: 15 minutes after we went upstairs two Israeli soldiers approached the house, looked in the cellar and threw two hand grenades in. Many were injured: two girls, aged 12 and 14, were killed. The soldiers then asked all the survivors to come out and they blindfolded the men and lined them up on the wall. A soldier hit a heavily pregnant woman from the Al Bitar family from Khan Younis camp with the back of his gun. Her husband said to him, 'Don't you have any mercy?' The soldier replied, 'I will show you mercy.' He took him away behind the trees, then everyone heard the sound of two bullets: the man was killed.

Fortunately, the same Ben-Gurion orders were received and executions were stopped. My grandmother decided to go back to our house in Khan Younis immediately, even before the ceasefire was announced. To her what her grandchildren witnessed was horrific enough. She walked with my brothers and sisters, all holding hands and preparing for the worst. As they arrived at the main town square, there were dozens of bodies in front of the castle, swimming in their blood (in the words of my sister Mai). My grandmother started to look at each body, turning some of them over and crying loudly. My brother and sisters thought it was very strange as the scene was horrific and all of them wanted to get home quickly, but this was my grandmother's way of grieving for them and their families.

Out of the horrific tragedy came some funny stories. My late cousin Kamal was only 18 when the Israeli soldiers arrived at our street in Khan Younis. They took all the male residents of our street to the town square in front of the castle. With them was our neighbour Abdullah Wadi, who owned the most famous spice shop in the area. He was so trusted by people from the neighbourhood and beyond that it was thought only his spices could produce good food. His herbal treatment for many illnesses was the only viable one in the eyes of most locals. On many occasions other spice shop owners pretended they were him to get business from unsuspecting people from outside the town. He had one of the sweetest senses of humour.

When it came to their turn the soldiers lined them up on the wall of the castle. Kamal was next to Uncle Abdullah. Kamal was as terrified as everyone else. They both were reciting their last prayers. When they finished Kamal asked Uncle Abdullah innocently, 'What are they going to do with us?' Shocked at the question, Uncle Abdullah stood up despite the great risk and started dancing and singing, 'They are going to take us to a party, we are going to dance till we drop.' The soldiers told him off. They all laughed and this story has become part of our neighbourhood lore, to be retold generation after generation. My late Uncle Abdulsallam told it to me; he always laughed his head off when he did.

Uncle Abdulsallam was standing next to them facing the wall. He always wore a suit with a fez on his head. One soldier came and took the fez off his head and dropped it on the floor. My uncle would pick it up and put it on again; the soldier would come and take it off again. This was repeated many times. Then my uncle told the soldier, 'You are going to kill me so what difference does it make if I am wearing the fez or not?'

As they were all waiting for the executions to be carried out, an Israeli jeep arrived with the orders from the Israeli Prime Minister Ben-Gurion to stop the killing (as the news of the massacre had started to reach the UN officials in the Gaza Strip). The last round of executions did not take place: my uncle, Kamal and Uncle Abdullah survived at the very last stage. They were without a doubt the lucky ones. They lived to tell us their story and the horrific ones of others. They all returned to their houses apart from one of my relatives, Qasem Saeed El Farra, who went to check on his uncle, Abu Asaad. Less than a hundred metres away from the castle walls, he was met by a group of soldiers who shot him dead on the spot.

One of the most infuriating aspects of being a Palestinian is that although the picture of more than 64 years of ethnic cleansing of our race is crystal clear to anyone who is interested – despite occupation and denial of every basic Palestinian human right – we have to continue to justify our suffering, and just demands. We have to continue to try to persuade a sizeable section of international public opinion that we are the oppressed in this conflict rather than the oppressor.

The Khan Younis massacre in 1956 is another clear example of the hugely powerful Zionist propaganda machine which has always been followed by most of the Western media. Many famous pro-Israeli scholars and intellectuals, although they may have a reasonable stand on the issue of Palestine, rush to support the Israeli version of most events. When reviewing Noam Chomsky's book *The Fateful Triangle* in the *New York Review of Books*, Avishai Margalit, an American professor of philosophy, reacted angrily to Chomsky's mention of the Khan Younis massacre (28 June 1984).

In his reply Chomsky wrote:

> Margalit has two objections to my reference to this massacre. First, he says that "knowledgeable Israeli sources" believe that the 275 figure "is too high." Second, "What is missing from this account, however, is the fact that each of the persons who were shot was identified as a Fedayeen (or terrorist, in Israel's current jargon)…" [*NYRB*, June 28]. The UNRWA reports and Moshe Dayan's, a Former Israeli Defense Minister, diaries deny this claim.
>
> Here is what I wrote: "The Israeli occupying army carried out bloody atrocities in the Gaza Strip, killing at least 275 Palestinians immediately after capturing the Strip during a brutal house-to-house search for weapons and fedayeen in Khan Younis. Margalit agrees that these 'executions' were 'evil.' One may imagine the reaction had Israelis been slaughtered in this manner by an Arab army after an attack on Israel."
>
> It is an unfortunate fact that occupying armies often behave in this fashion but then, they usually do not bask in the admiration of American intellectuals for their unique and remarkable commitment to purity of arms.
>
> Knowledgeable Israeli sources have been notoriously unreliable, with regard to their own atrocities. Recall, for example, Ben-Gurion's pretence that the 1953 Qibya massacre was not committed by the IDF,[16]

---

[16] The Qibya massacre occurred in October 1953 when Israeli troops under Ariel Sharon attacked the village of Qibya in the West Bank. Sixty-nine Palestinian Arabs, two-thirds of them women and children, were killed. Forty-five houses, a school, and a mosque were destroyed. The act was condemned by the US State Department, the UN Security Council, and by Jewish communities worldwide. The operation was

or Moshe Sharett's[17] outraged denial of Egyptian charges concerning Israeli terrorism in Egypt in 1954 (which he knew to be accurate), and so on until the present, e.g., Israel's official claim that 340 civilians only were killed and 40 buildings destroyed in the bombing of Beirut in 1982.[18]

(cont.) codenamed Operation Shoshana by the Israel Defense Force (IDF). It was carried out by two Israeli units at night: a paratroop company and Unit 101, a Special Forces unit of the IDF. (www.encyclo.co.uk)

[17] Moshe Sharett was the second Prime Minister of Israel (1953–55), serving for a little under two years between David Ben-Gurion's two terms.

[18] *1982 Israeli invasion of Lebanon* After invading southern Lebanon four years earlier, Israel launched a massive attack on 6 June 1982. Israel called its 1982 invasion 'Operation Peace for Galilee'. Its stated aim was to force the Palestinian Liberation Organization (PLO) out of Lebanon. Throughout the 1970s and early 1980s the PLO used guerilla tactics to fight Israel.

On 3 June 1982 members of Abu Nidal's anti-PLO militia made an assassination attempt on Israel's ambassador to the United Kingdom, Shlomo Argov. Israel ignored overwhelming evidence that showed the PLO was not responsible for the failed assassination attempt and invaded southern Lebanon. Israel invaded with an army of 76,000 troops, 800 tanks, 1,500 armored personnel carriers and 634 airplanes.

As a result of the invasion, 17,825 Lebanese were killed, over 30,000 were injured as well as roughly 9,797 Syrian and PLO fighters. 675 Israeli soldiers died in the invasion.

The PLO forces negotiated passage from Lebanon with the aid of Special Envoy Philip Habib and the protection of international peacekeepers. Habib issued a guarantee from the US administration that the Palestinian civilians within the camps would be protected as well.

The worst incident of the 1982 invasion came between 16 and 18 September, when former Israeli Defense Minister Ariel Sharon allowed Christian Maronite Phalangist militiamen to massacre over 1,000 Palestinian civilians in the refugee camps, Sabra and Shatila. According to several reports Sharon gave the Phalangists carte blanche to enter the camps. Israeli forces fired flares over the camps at night to aid the Phalangist gunmen.

Following the fall of Khan Younis on the sixth day of the 1967 war, locals thought that what had happened in 1956 would be repeated. Two hundred and seventy thousand Palestinians from the West Bank and the Gaza Strip fled to Jordan and Egypt fearing for their lives; others left their homes and went into hiding by the seashore waiting for the news.

Just before the start of the Israeli attack on Egypt, Syria and Jordan in 1967, the Egyptian army leadership took a decision to swap units of the Palestinian Liberation Army Special Forces (*Al Sa'iqah*) between different towns in the Gaza Strip.[19] As a result, the *Al Sa'iqah* unit from Gaza City was placed in Khan Younis and vice versa. They did not know the town at all. Their leader, Major Abu Sha'ban, was a friend of my father. He asked him to help them as a guide: my father did not hesitate for a moment. My father guided them through streets and alleys over six days of intense fighting with the invading Israel army. All the family are extremely proud of his contribution.

Before the war my father joined the popular resistance groups training programme at the Palestine Liberation Army camps run by the Egyptian army. The aim was to train them to defend different neighbourhoods in the Gaza Strip in case of an Israeli attack.

I was 6 years old in 1967. I remember clearly my father inviting

---

(cont.)The Israeli Kahan investigation committee into Sabra and Shatila found that Sharon was guilty of failing to prevent the death of hundreds, maybe even thousands, of innocent civilians. Despite the investigations findings, Sharon would go on to become the Prime Minister of Israel. (Ma'an News Agency)

[19] The Palestine Liberation Army was established by Ahmad Shoqairi, the founder and first chairman of the Palestine Liberation Organization, 1964–67. At the 1964 Arab League summit, he was given a mandate to initiate contacts aimed at establishing a Palestinian entity. In May 1964, he was elected the first chairman of the PLO (Palestine Liberation Organization). He resigned in December 1967 in the aftermath of the Six-Day War in June. Shukeiri was succeeded as Chairman of PLO by Yahya Hammuda, who was then succeeded by Yasser Arafat. He died in 1980 in Jordan.

some of the *Sa'iqa* fighters to use the rooftop of our house to fight the invading Israeli troops. Our house was one of a few houses in Khan Younis more than one storey high. It had a cellar with thick walls that my father had built fearing wars like these. My mother screamed her head off asking him not to let them use it. He tried to push her aside and let them in but she would not budge. 'Are you crazy?' she said. 'We have more than sixty neighbours and relatives hiding in the basement: do you want them to destroy the house on top of us?' Finally it clicked and my father apologized politely to his comrades.

Following the fall of Khan Younis, my father went upstairs, put his best suit and his best aftershave on, and started whistling and singing. My mother begged him to come down to the cellar as the shelling was still taking place. Initially he refused, but he had to when my mother got hysterical – as she always did in circumstances like these. He told her he was preparing to meet his creator looking the best he could or, if arrested, to face them looking as elegant and as graceful as he could. My father was not joking: we were waiting for the killing to start exactly as it had in 1956. Happily, it did not happen this time.

Khan Younis residents are so proud our town fell to the Israeli army on the sixth day of the war while all other fronts fell on the first. The resistance forces carried out a truly heroic battle, as documented by Israeli historians. Our house witnessed an historic meeting between my father and the leader of the *Al Sa'iqa* force in the Khan Younis area, Major Abu Shaban. At this meeting Major Abu Shaban handed my father a bullet. 'This is the last bullet my forces have,' he said. 'Had it not been for this we would have continued to resist. Please, Qasem, remember this to everyone.' I recall clearly my father taking my brother Mones and me to see the remains of the many Israeli army tanks destroyed in the Khan Younis battle in 1967. The occupation army pulled the remaining ones out of the city shortly after occupying it.

9

Ibrahim, Kassab, Shakespeare and Dickens

The following morning, I was very nervous during the journey from Khan Younis to Al Fukhari to meet Muhammad Shurab (Abu Absal). I had followed the details of the killing of his two sons, Kassab (28) and Ibrahim (18), on different satellite channels but the idea of listening to his story set off turbulent emotions within me. I have known the family since I was a child. His younger brother Ibrahim Abu Khalil has been a good friend of mine for years. Muhammad worked hard in UAE for thirty years. In the nineties he returned to settle in Khan Younis. In 1997 he bought a piece of land right on the border with Israel. He built numerous beehives in the middle of his almond and olive grove and started a small honey production business to support his family. Muhammad's house is not far from the main border gate with Israel at the end of the Al Fukhari area. Muhammad and his family, being close to the watch-tower at the gate, were well known to the Israeli army.

Muhammad met us outside the house. I was expecting to meet a broken man: on the contrary, he greeted us with a wide smile; a well-informed graceful man who can still joke and exchange funny stories despite what he has experienced.

'I was aware Israeli army units were in the area,' Muhammad said. 'I could see them every day from my house; they also could see me clearly. I did not think much of it when I decided to go to Khan Younis during the ceasefire from 10 a.m. to 2 p.m. one Friday. I had done this the previous two Fridays, since the beginning of the war. After all, it was the Israeli army who declared the ceasefire: hence, why should I expect anything bad to happen? My two sons, Kassab and Ibrahim, were with me. I wanted to join the rest of my family as I always did at the weekend. I picked our departure time carefully: 12 noon. By then, two peaceful hours of the ceasefire have passed which is always a good indication. I drove my civilian Land Rover very slowly. It was a sunny day – otherwise I would not have taken this journey. Kassab was in the front seat and Ibrahim in the back.

'I passed an Israeli tank on the side of the road; it was partially hidden behind two sand dunes. I waved at the tank, saying "Salam Alaikum" which is "Peace upon you" in Arabic. The tanks did not stop us. I had driven for about 50 metres when suddenly, without any warning, the Israeli soldiers started firing heavily at my car. I said to my sons, "Get down, get down!" The firing continued. My left arm was hit. Then the soldiers started shouting, "Get out of the car, you son of a bitch!" I could not control the car: I crashed into a wall. Kassab came out of the car with both hands in the air. It was clear he was unarmed. He took no more than five steps then they shot him directly, seven times in the chest: shoot to kill.

'Ibrahim and I were hit when we were still in the car. Ibrahim's left leg was injured. As we got out, I saw Kassab. He was flat on his front, not moving. There were only five steps between me and Kassab.

'Ibrahim kept shouting, "Baba, don't worry, my injury is not serious, it is below the knee. I need an ambulance." The soldiers shouted, "Shut up or I will finish you off!" We crawled towards the wall nearby. Ibrahim tried to phone 101 to get an ambulance. One of the soldiers shouted, "Drop your mobile phone or I will kill you!" Ibrahim had to comply and continued to bleed. Every time we tried to make a phone call they threatened to shoot. After approximately an hour, I didn't care. I phoned for a Palestinian ambulance: they told me only Red Cross ambulances can get through but the Israeli army was refusing them a permit to reach us.

'I continued to phone more than twenty times. They asked me to keep my mobile free so the press could contact me. I appealed through local radio, TV stations and other satellite stations for help:

but to no avail. I noticed cats and dogs moving around Kassab's body. I started crawling towards him despite threats from the soldiers. His body was frozen. I realized then that he was dead. I covered his face with his jacket. I said to myself, "At least Ibrahim is still alive."

'It got dark, the weather was very cold. Ibrahim asked me to take him back to the car for warmth. As we started to move, one of the Israeli soldiers shouted, "Stop, I will kill you if you move!" I put Ibrahim's head on my lap. I started shouting hysterically, "Oh, you so-called civilized people, you the grandsons of Abraham, my son Ibrahim is bleeding, he is dying, you killed my son Kassab. If you have any drop of humanity, get us an ambulance." The answer was always the same, "Shut up or I will kill you."'

Muhammad's brother Ibrahim (whom Muhammad's son was named after when he was in an Israeli prison) sat next to him remembering, 'I did not know what happened until I phoned my nephew Ibrahim at approximately 1 p.m. on his mobile when I thought that they were late. Ibrahim told me what had happened, sounding petrified. I went with a Red Crescent ambulance on Friday afternoon. When we were about a hundred metres from the tanks the soldiers directed their barrels at the ambulance. The ambulance driver was terrified. They shouted aggressively, "Have you got permission from the Israeli army coordination unit?" We did not have permission: we had to go back. I felt furious. My brother and my nephew are no more than a hundred metres away and I cannot reach them: how humiliating is this I wonder? At 5 p.m. I received a very disappointing phone call from the Red Crescent: there is no hope of sending an ambulance, they said.'

'Ibrahim was shivering on my lap. I was also very cold,' Muhammad continued. 'All we could hear was the bulldozers demolishing houses and raising agricultural land in the area. At this stage I was virtually covered with my blood and Ibrahim's. We were only a kilometre away from the European hospital, one of the biggest hospitals in the Gaza Strip, yet we could not even move a step towards it.

'At about 11:30 Ibrahim started to feel even colder. I kept massaging his back to keep him warm. I shouted hysterically at the soldiers, "If you do not want the ambulances to reach us then please give us a blanket," but to no avail. Ibrahim tied some dirty underwear on his head. He started to have difficulty breathing; he stopped talking. At midnight he stopped breathing; I touched his face. At this moment, I realized I had lost both of them. I realized he was dead. Before he died he kept repeating, "Baba, are you happy with me? I want you to be, I don't want to die leaving you upset about anything I have done." I kept saying to him, "Of course I am happy with you."

'All through these long painful hours Ibrahim kept asking about his brother. "I want to follow Kassab," he kept saying. I think Ibrahim died feeling sad about Kassab. He was his mentor, he taught him everything; they were very close brothers. I was so proud of them.

'At 1 a.m. I received the first phone call from a Tom Mhajir from Physicians for Human Rights Israel (PHRI). He kept phoning until the early hours in the morning when the battery of my mobile ran out. He kept promising to help. I told him, "Tom, it is over, my two sons are dead. Now I need help to move their bodies. I am dying. If we were dogs in Israel or any Western country, they would not treat us this way." Tom tried his best but to no avail.

'I continued to wait bleeding while hugging the bodies of my two sons until late morning on the following day, 17 January, when the ambulances were allowed by the Israeli army to reach me: approximately twenty-three hours after we were fired upon.

'The Israeli army had civilian hostages in a house near where we were shot. A senior Israeli army officer had a call from the soldiers within the special unit which fired on us. They informed him a car with three civilians was approaching. He ordered them to open fire on the car, which was ours. How did I know? One of my labourers was a hostage himself. He spoke Hebrew and understood the conversation.

'I am still partially paralyzed. I need a lot of treatment. I still cannot get the transfer. My spinal cord is partially paralyzed. I continue to have a lot of pain in my hand. I need professional medical treatment which unfortunately does not exist in the Gaza Strip.

'I have a herd of sheep; Ibrahim loved to look after them, feed them and wash them. He loved the place; he had a cat he loved dearly; he named it Latifa ['gentle' in Arabic]. Having been an accountant for more than thirty years, I used to teach Ibrahim commerce. He was an outstanding student: he secured a scholarship because of his brilliance. He was studying economics at Al Azhar University. His teachers always said he was exceptional, ahead of his age. I sacrificed a lot for their well-being and education. Maybe it is strange to say but I feel the loss of Ibrahim more than anything.'

Muhammad picked a file from his well-organized library. He showed me the graduation project of his late son Kassab who graduated as an architect from the Islamic university in Gaza. Proudly he went through the different parts of the project. Being an engineer myself I was able to recognize it as a high quality project. 'Kassab was also clever,' Muhammad sighed. 'I wish I could live to build a mem-orial for Kassab and Ibrahim.'

'Kassab had plans to get married. We were all happy about this. He was 28 years old when he was killed: this is the usual age for men to get married in our society. I am left with two boys and two girls. We were relying a lot on Kassab and Ibrahim to help the family. In our culture the parents support the children, then the children support the family.

'Kassab and Ibrahim had a close relationship with the family,' Muhammad recounted. 'They were keen on developing their skills. They were very good readers; they read more than five hundred books in my library: Shakespeare and Charles Dickens and many others.

'This taught me a lot not to rush anything: I try to see the good in everyone. I think what happened to our family dwarfed everything else, relatively speaking.

'Nothing can compensate me for the loss of my beloved Kassab and Ibrahim. Nobody seems to care anymore.

'I do not think that life will go on as usual. I am worried what is coming is worst, I am not optimistic at all. In 2009 we lost more than 1,400 martyrs. I think if they could kill us all they would do it.

'I did not realize how weak and vulnerable we are until I suffered what I suffered. They are vicious. I did not think that anybody could do what they did to me and my kids. Their mother is still suffering frequent nervous breakdowns. She goes into crying fits five or six times a day; we try to avoid any mention of them. She suffers from epilepsy. She has had 120 sessions of psychiatric treatment. She is mentally and physically damaged, not the mother or the woman she used to be. She wants to read the Quran all the time. It affected her relationship with my two daughters.

'My daughters are still very shaken by what happened. On one occasion, I took one of them to hospital as she was suffering from swelling. When she came back, she suddenly started shouting: "Ibrahim, where is Ibrahim? I want him now." This was in August 2009, seven months after the killing of my sons. My kids did not belong to any organization. They were the children of Palestine: this is how I would love them to be remembered.

'The loss of Kassab and Ibrahim feels like severe damage to all my organs: it will never heal. Immediately afterwards, I felt that killing the entire population of Israel would compensate me for this. However, going back to my senses, I remembered how I used to think before this tragedy: what would the killing of anybody do for me? What about the good people who do not associate themselves with such war crimes? What about my friend, Amira Oron, and many other friends from Israel still phoning me? They are innocent. What about that friendly young man Tom from PHRI who did his best to help us? He comes from the same country and background as the soldiers who killed my beloved sons. Tom and people like him represent the humanity I expect of our neighbors. As for those soldiers my feelings remain different.

'Yesterday, we fed the animals. It was a sunny day like this, just like when Kassab and Ibrahim were brutally taken away from us. Everything was lovely around here: not anymore.'

Sadly, Muhmmad's health and psychological condition continued to deteriorate. He passed away in September, 2012.

10

Tales of Al Zaytoun

My next set of visits was in Al Zaytoun area which suffered a great deal during the Israeli ground invasion following the air bombardment. Al Zaytoun in Arabic means 'olives'; it was named after the vast olive groves there. There are very few left due to the ongoing increase of population which transformed the beautiful olive groves to a heavily populated area. The continual Israeli destruction of agricultural land has also caused the loss of the olive and orange groves.

Omar Al Mukhtar, the longest street in Gaza City, starts near the centre of Al Zaytoun, and extends more than two kilometres to the west, all the way to the Mediterranean. It was here at Al Zaytoun I had one of the most exciting sporting experiences of my teenage years. I represented my town, Khan Younis Sports Club, at the 1977 Table Tennis championships, which was held at the Al Ahli sports club at the heart of Al Zaytoun. At that time, despite the occupation and a severe shortage of space and equipment, Palestinians tried their best to take part in sport. Al Ahli Sports Club, like many others, was established in a tiny flat but then developed over the years to become one of the established sports clubs in Gaza. I battled players from all over the Gaza Strip to win the silver medal in the individual tournament. I also won the silver medal in the club tournaments alongside my friends, Jamal and Al Jourany.

My reminiscing was brought short by my arrival at the house of Nabawiyah Al Samouny (34) in a deprived part of Al Zaytoun. She was sitting down, hugging her 14-month-old daughter Islam. The overcrowding, the unpaved narrow streets and the dozens of poorly clad children playing outside makes the residents' hardship clear.

'I had to sell my own sewing machine to help with Islam's treatment,' Nabawiyah sighed with great sadness. 'I sold my wedding ring to buy Islam her medical boots. We also borrowed from many people. I will do everything to treat my daughter. She is clever and very sweet, I will not abandon her no matter what.'

'I have 10 children, six girls and four boys. I love them all but I can say confidently that Islam is the dearest to my heart. She suffered and is suffering since birth for no reason, none whatsoever. The images of the thick white smoke can never leave my mind. This has become part of my never-ending nightmare. It is also in a way part of Islam's tragic condition although she did not see it.

'In January 2009, they attacked us with white phosphorus bombs. I was three months pregnant with Islam. We were inside our house. The whole neighbourhood was full of smoke. The grain fields nearby were on fire. Many houses were also on fire.

'There were so many injured. The Israeli army phoned many times ordering us to leave our houses but where can we go? The smoke from the phosphorus bombs was too much for me to take. I fainted and fell down, many times. I asked my husband to look after the kids. I thought that I was dying. My husband also said his prayers. My kids hid below the beds, it was too terrifying. This happened during the night. It was nonstop shelling, but we did not leave our house.

'They cut off the water and electricity. Then came the phone call with their most serious threat ordering us to leave or they will bomb the house. They repeated this threat to most of the houses. It was then that we decided to leave. Almost everyone in Al Zaytoun Al Sharqi started to leave their houses at the same time. My husband carried me and we left the house.'

Ahmad, Nabawiyah's 13-year-old son, remembered the Israeli Apaches even bombing a fruit stall. 'How crazy was that?' he said.

'We fled to Asqoolah school. We took nothing from the house, only a few blankets, travelling on a donkey and a cart belonging to my brother-in-law. I was barefoot. There were people fleeing everywhere in all directions, some of the refugees from the area said that it felt the 1948 Nakba was happening again.

'Many people were injured and killed while fleeing. The Apache helicopters were on top of us. It was obvious we were civilians fleeing but yet they attacked us. I do not know why.

'We stayed for 15 days at the school. We were 45 people hiding in one classroom. It felt as if the whole of Al Zaytoun Al Sharqi had left their homes. It was very undignified. We were sleeping crammed next to each other like sardines in a tin. The toilets were dirty; no water; no electricity.

'The situation was terrible. A lot of children suffered stomach problems and flu. It took only one child to have something to pass it to the rest. Each family received six pita breads per day from the UNRWA. I received no medical attention during this period. Before the war I used to have regular check-ups during my pregnancies.

'The war ended and we returned home. I fell ill. I was unable to move my left arm and left leg. I also had pain in my neck. The doctors told me that this was triggered by my fall when I fainted. I also need major surgery to treat my hip. I was ill all the time after the war. I had to keep visiting doctors.

'When Islam was born her legs were wrapped around each other, she had malformation in the hip and the joints. Her toes were permanently clenched. She has had five operations since the war; she has improved a lot but she is still not able to stand on her feet. She suffers a lot of pain at night-time. She had her first operation when she was 14 days old.

'The doctors treating her confirmed it was due to my inhalation of white phosphorus. She is the only child among all my children who suffers from this condition. All of them were born normal.

'I wish to live to see a day when these criminals are brought to justice. They destroyed the life of my baby, Islam, even before she was born. I also lost three brothers in the same war, Talal, Rashad and Atia, and their wives, Rabab, Laila and Rahma and their kids during the attacks on my family's compound, the Al Samouny compound, not far from us to the east.

'My brothers were very kind; they always supported me. Life feels empty without them. This piece of carpet was a present from them. My husband is very poor; they frequently brought me jam, cheese, fruit and vegetables. They gave me money. They even gave me all this without my husband knowing. They were so keen not to hurt his feelings since he was a poor man: this is how great and sensitive they were. My mother, Shifa Al Samouny, was under the rubble for three days; she was among the missing. She still cannot walk, she has a disability from her injury – she still has shrapnel in her arms and legs. I always tell my son Ahmad that school is better than working to help his father. He always replies, "How else will we survive?" Now I cannot help my husband, and with the cost of living and Islam's treatment, Ahmad thinks there is no choice but to leave school and work with his father on the donkey and cart. This is another side of how they destroyed not only our present but the future of our children. I cannot help it but my heart is filled with hatred for whatever they represent and whoever supports them. I am not proud of this but these are my true feelings.

'I hope the day will come when I will be able to forget but it feels impossible at present. My brothers, their wives, my cousins, the suffering of my mother and baby daughter: it is too much to tolerate.'

A short distance down the road is the Wadi family house. Many houses in the neighbourhood still have holes, both small and large, caused by bullets and missiles. Entering the Wadi home you immediately experience true Gazan warmth and friendliness – despite the harsh conditions the family live under.

'You'll have to excuse me for a minute,' said Muayad Abu Wadi, while his wife Samahir (30) welcomed us with a big smile. 'I have to borrow some chairs from the neighbours.'

'We share this house with my two brothers, and their families. Each family lives in one room. We could not afford to build an extension,' he said.

'The Wadi family comes originally from the town of Beer al-Saba in the southern part of Palestine.[20]

---

[20] Beer al-Saba (Beersheba) is a small, modern town, 71 kilometres southwest of Jerusalem. Beer al-Saba was conquered on 20–21 October 1948

'Since the beginning of the ground attack on 3 January 2009, the Israeli army had bombed our area with great intensity. They even attacked two nearby mosques. We had to leave the house as a result of the continuous shelling. We went to my Uncle Nayif's house which is very close. We thought it was safer. After we left, a few shells landed outside our house causing a lot of damage to the walls and windows. The cupboards, television and fridge were destroyed. The kitchen was also badly damaged. When we saw this we thought we'd made the right decision: after all, we were alive and that is what mattered to us.'

'The next day I went up to the flat roof together with some female relatives,' Samahir recounted. 'There were about 20 of us. We started baking for all the families hiding in the flats below. When we had finished I stayed on top of the roof while the other women went downstairs. My cousin Mirvat stayed with me.

'At one o'clock in the afternoon my 7-year-old son Baha was playing on the roof with his brothers and sisters. He asked for lots of food. He looked very happy; he was singing. He asked me for one Israeli shekel to go out and buy sweets. I put my hand in my pocket to get the money. I heard what sounded like breaking glass. I did not know what had happened. I looked for him: he was on the floor and blood was everywhere. He had been hit in the back of his head which was split in half. I carried him: he was bleeding heavily. I tried to keep his brains inside his skull. My Uncle Nayif came with a group of relatives. I screamed, "My son is dead." They rushed him to hospital but he was already dead.'

(cont.) with the use of aerial bombardment. The vast majority of Beer al-Saba population were forcibly removed. The conquering of Beer al-Saba was part of Operation Yoav. It was headed by Southern Front commander Yigal Allon, and in its course all the residents of the following villages were conquered and expelled: al-Khalasa, Bayt Tima, Dimra, Beit Jirja, Dayr Sunayd, Hiribya, al-Majdal, Barbara, Hamama, al-Jiyya, al-Khisas, Ni'ilya, Iraq Suwaydan, Iraq al-Manshiyya, Ajjur, Kudna, Ra'na, Zikrin, Dayr al-Dubban, al-Qubayba, Khirbat Umm Burj, Beit Jibrin, al-Dawayima, Dayr Al-Nakhkhas, and al-Jura. (www.zochorot.org)

'I wanted to follow him to the hospital,' Muayad said. 'Everyone tried to stop me. It was not safe, they were targeting everything, civilians, cars, everything. I could not go; they brought his body back. We went to bury him. Only five people came: people were too scared to leave their houses even for an emotional thing like burying Baha, an innocent child. We were told afterwards Baha was hit on the head by an object believed to be a rocket from a reconnaissance aircraft or a tank.

'After that, we had to flee to the UN schools, as things got worst. We stayed in a school classroom for three weeks.

'I work as a labourer and Samahir is a full-time housewife,' he continued. 'We could not afford to even replace the curtains or the cupboard. We are poor people who were punished on top of that. The kids used to enjoy sleeping overnight at their grandparents' house: they did this frequently. Now, if we ask them if they wish to go and sleep there, they refuse. They are still scared: they keep saying that if they are going to die they prefer to die with us. A week ago the Israeli army bombed our area. They woke up terrified and clung to me and their mother.

'Baha was mischievous; brighter than his brothers and sisters. He loved cats; we had so many cats. We try to keep them inside the house. He loved going to the funfair; he always asked his mum, "When is Eid? I want to go to the funfair."

'Baha's brother Ziyad (9) is still in a state of shock. He saw Baha when he died. He saw the blood. Only last night he woke up crying loudly for no reason. He cannot forget the scene he saw. He started not concentrating at school. The school called me. I went there and they complained he is not achieving. I explained he is still in shock from the killing of his brother. He is always ill and weak; I often take him to hospital. His way of thinking is not the same; he is not balanced any more. My other kids could have been killed in the same attack: thank goodness they were not.

'My wife is still shaken two years after the attack. She never forgets Baha – she loves all her kids but she always saw Baha as a special boy.

'He loved to play all kinds of games. He was just an ordinary child. He loved to watch *Tom and Jerry* cartoons. He always cried when we changed the channel. He also loved an Arabic cartoon,

Karamish. Every time his brothers and sisters watch this programme they remember Baha and end up in tears. We always feel sad when we watch it. I do not want his brothers and sisters to stop watching it. I hope they will forget one day: life must go on.

'We have a strong feeling this attack was deliberate: why else with all their sophisticated weapons would they target a child like Baha? They want to kill all the Palestinians.

'They behave as if their superiority will last forever but it will not. In history all the big empires built on tyranny and aggression have been destroyed and this will happen to them.'

'I always think about when he played with his brothers and sisters,' Samahir said. 'When they play now I watch them and immediately think, "Oh my God, Baha is missing."

11

Olympic dreams

Still in Eastern Zaytoun, I didn't have to travel far to be met by a large friendly smile from 23-year-old Muhammad Totah.

Muhammad spent hours each day after work training hard to fulfil his dream. The only thing on his mind was to obtain a black belt in karate and continue until he was good enough to represent Palestine in the Olympic Games. The image of him carrying the Palestinian flag in the opening ceremony never left his mind.

'This was my ultimate dream,' Muhammad said. 'I achieved the blue belt and I was confident I would get the black belt. My trainer was also convinced it was only a matter of time before I would do so. I was very excited about the whole idea: me, Muhammad, a young man from the poor area, Al Zaytoun Al Sharqi, in Gaza, rubbing shoulders with the athletes of the world. Wow, what an awesome dream!'

Muhammad's aunt phoned on 27 December 2008, the first day of the Israeli attacks on the Gaza Strip. She was terrified. The shelling had intensified where she lived in Gaza City. She asked for someone to keep her company. Her husband was on duty at Al Wafa hospital: he could not leave his work because of the emergency and the high number of casualties from the Israeli bombing. Muhammad did not hesitate for a minute. After all, that was his nature, to be extremely kind to all members of his family and others.

'I arrived at my auntie's house. In the afternoon my family phoned from home: the power was cut off. They asked for help as they could not start the generator. They were worried my young brothers and sisters would be scared when night fell. On the way back, when the rockets started falling near Tunis school, I was hit by the shrapnel. I was conscious for nearly half an hour. The ambulances could not reach me because the shelling continued. I elevated my right leg. I screamed, asking people for a blanket. I was very cold. They brought me a blanket. I was conscious until I reached Al Shifa hospital. As I arrived the Israeli army attacked nearby. I was at the ER; people around me were terrified. The doctors operated on me: my right leg had to be amputated. My heart stopped for seven minutes in hospital. After I got hit, I kept feeling my body parts: my hands, my head, my legs. I realized then that there was something wrong with my right leg. I realized because of the severity of the injury I would lose my leg. The doctors said to my father that it was because of elevating my leg that I did not die: my blood would have dried out.

'I was in a coma for two days then I woke up on the third day. I was very thirsty and I stretched out my hand to ask for water. I found out that both hands were severely injured. I was very distressed because I thought I would lose my hands as well as the leg I had lost already.

'The amputation was about 25 centimetres above the right knee. Unfortunately, the artificial limb I have is giving me a lot of pain: it is not suitable for my injury. I am very upset about that.

'After the injury, the National Society for Rehabilitation (NSR) helped me cope with my new situation. After all, my life changed from normal to that of a disabled person. I started visiting the NSR and took part in many courses and activities. I helped with the preparation for the summer camps which was a fantastic experience. I joined in with lots of things. I used to be very good at table tennis before the injury. I still play – I took part in a tournament organized for the disabled. I came second: I was proud of this. I also helped to plant trees replacing those destroyed by the Israeli army at Al Thamaniyah Street in Gaza. All the trees were planted by victims who lost limbs. There was a philosophy behind this. They severed my leg: I wanted to plant something in the earth instead of my leg which I could not plant again.

'I took part in swimming and day trips. I finished a course in maintenance for mobile phones. I would be happy to start my own mobile phone business, but financially I cannot. No one cares for us as a priority. This is sad.

'I am an independent Palestinian who belongs to Palestine. I feel I am ignored by the Palestinian leadership.

'I still feel the pain psychologically. On the anniversary of the war, I felt very sad; I remembered what happened to me. It made me very depressed. The pain intensifies when it is cold. I scream loudly when I have the pain.

'I have nothing against the Israeli people who objected to this criminal war. I welcome all the solidarity work at Billin and other areas in the West Bank. Some Jews take part in these actions against Israeli atrocities: this is good to see.

'Since the injury, I constantly suffer from lack of sleep. I do not feel like having fun as I used to before. I lose my temper quickly, my personality has changed. I feel I am a burden on my family, I feel very upset I cannot support myself or my pregnant wife. I am thinking of my unborn baby and how to get strong to be able to support him or her.

'I never lose hope: in the middle of my dire situation, I always try to be positive. I like Palestinian folklore, I find it therapeutically beneficial for me to get over my problems momentarily. I love to sing Palestinian melodies.' Muhammad then started singing 'Ya maijana w yamaijana'; beautiful lyrics about the warmth and generosity of the Palestinians, our love of life despite all the tragedies we go through. 'I sing for the fields of Palestine, let's plant, let's harvest, let's sing for the children of Palestine. I feel for the children in Palestine and Iraq. They see nothing but fire and tanks. It is sad: I hope that one day they will have a better life.

'Sometimes I remember the days when I used to do karate and I feel sad. Last week, someone told me that in Western countries people with a disability can still practise a lot of sports, including karate. I felt very happy about that. I will enquire with the Palestinian Karate Association about it. I doubt it will be available here in Gaza but if I keep persisting maybe they will consider it. This will be a really great thing if I can manage it.

'Can you see what happened to me? My dream has changed from wanting to be an Olympic champion to being able to support myself. No complaints: this is what it was meant to be . . . although sometimes I ask, "Why should this happen to me?"'

12

Combing my daughters' hair is impossible

For Najah Dadir El Ghiffary, a 42-year-old housewife from Eastern Zaytoun, family was her whole life. After all, she did not get any further education after high school. She got married very young and had 11 children, six boys and five girls. Looking after them gave her a sense of purpose. Then, her husband Hassan fell ill with hepatitis B. He could not continue to work. Life became much more difficult. Najah used to help to support the family by spending a few hours each week refurbishing furniture cushions and mattreses, and embroidering pillow covers. Now her husband was ill the full responsibility fell on her to support the family. Najah did not mind and did this without any complaint.

'On 8 January 2009, following the Israeli army ground attack, the resistance fighters launched a rocket on Israel from our area.' Najah's eyes were full of sadness as she talked. 'The Israeli army retaliated by launching an indiscriminate air attack on the whole area. The drones and Apaches started to hover over us. Before sunset our house was attacked with two rockets from the air. We were inside. One rocket landed at the front of the house. We felt the house shaking. We hid under the reinforced concrete staircase as it was the safest area. Shocked, I realized we had left two of my grandchildren, 16-month-old Hassan and the baby Malak, inside the house. Everyone was too terrified to go back to get them. I raised my courage and went back to the house to bring them out. I got out of the house carrying both of them back to where everyone was hiding under the staircase. The second rocket landed at the back of the house. We were hit by the shrapnel of the rockets: my two grandchildren were injured but miraculously their injuries were superficial. There was blood everywhere. I was in a state of shock. I did not realize what had happened to me; I did not even feel any pain until I saw my missing hand. I shouted hysterically, "Hassan, I lost my hand!" He came out and carried me. He walked into the street screaming for help.

'One of our neighbours offered his car to take me to hospital. At the hospital the doctors told me my right arm would have to be amputated. My jaw was hit severely; it was hanging down. I had to have many operations to rebuild it. I went to Saudi Arabia on the third day accompanied by my mother: I was not conscious. I came back after 16 days. When I woke up the doctor told me I was lucky to be alive. I also suffered severe injury to my shoulder.

'My youngest daughter Dua'a was 2 years old and Asma'a was 8. When they used to phone me in Saudi Arabia they always asked me to come back. When I came back they both were shocked. For days they would not come to me. My face made them scared. My jaw was swollen and my children could not understand what I said because I could not speak properly. My teeth were smashed inside my jaw. I had three operations to correct my jaw. I have improved a little bit but I still need special food. It has to be soft and blended; bread has to be wetted in tea.

'My son Ahmad is 13 years old; he was hit by two pieces of shrapnel, one in the leg and one in the face that penetrated the sinuses. Ahmad, a child who is now taking an adult's responsibility, showed a lot of dignity by telling me, "I have to work very hard to help my family. I go to the areas where the Israelis destroyed many buildings at Tal Al Hawa and Al Sabra. I take a donkey and a cart, collect big boulders of rubble and then break it with a big sledgehammer and an axe. Then I sieve through the rubble to segregate aggregates. I sell it to one of the local building contractors, a ready mixed concrete factory. Some days I earn 10 IS, others 15 IS." We want him to go to school but the situation is difficult. He feels it is his duty to help although it is so unfair on him: he is only a child,' Najah sighed. 'When I was working Ahmad used to go to school but now there is no option but to help the family. I am not happy about the situation at all but what can we do?'

'I find it very difficult to comb my daughters' hair after giving them a bath; it makes me feel very upset. I cannot even dress them. I feel terrible. I was very active before; I did everything around the house. I was alongside Hassan as a pillar of this house; not any more.

'Washing my kids' clothes is something that I cannot do any more; it is physically not possible as I used to do this manually. We cannot afford a washing machine. We'd rather buy food or clothes for our kids if we earn any money. This breaks my heart. My 14-year-old daughter has had to take on some of the housework. I feel sorry for her but we have no other choice.

'There were 11 injuries in the attack. My mother-in-law Samya Dadir, my sister-in-law Samahir, my two daughters Hanadi and Mai, my son Ahmad, and stepson Mahmoud, my daughter-in-law Laila; and our three grandchildren Hassan, Malak and Duaa.

'We were terrified when the TV announced Malak had been killed. The reason they said that is because she did not move for a long time so the people around her thought that she was dead. All the family and some friends rushed to hospital to get her body to prepare for the funeral. Instead, she was there alive. It was a nice surprise for all of them in the middle of the suffering they were going through.'

'We left the house after the attack,' Hassan recalls. 'We split into groups to stay with relatives. We took nothing with us other than our clothes; there was no time to think of taking anything. It was either we leave and live or stay and die.'

'My psychological condition is really terrible,' Najah continued. 'I feel my husband does not accept me any more. He says he does not mind me as I am. Some members of his family are putting pressure on him to marry another woman as I am disabled. Hassan helps me with a lot of things. He peels fruit for me as I find it very difficult to do so. But I have lost confidence: I do not think I am fit to be a partner to my husband now. He seems to be truthful in what he says but this is how I feel. I think it is a matter of time before he gets fed up with my situation since he is ill himself and needs attention. Our life has become such a misery on top of the poverty we suffered before all this.

'I still find it gruelling to cope with my current condition. I am disabled and there is no two ways about it. I was a person who had pride in helping my family. Now I am the one who needs help and from who? From my children who are not old enough to be responsible for something as difficult as looking after a disabled person.

'My kids are used to my situation; my relationship with them is almost back to normal. I still need corrective surgery to remove shrapnel from my shoulder. I am very worried and scared it may cause more damage. This worry has caused me regular lack of sleep. When I lay my head on the pillow, I can never stop thinking of what the future holds for me or my kids whom I love more than anything on earth.

'I frequently have nightmares. I wake up regularly, I remember what I was and what happened. I feel angry; I feel that for no reason my real me was taken away. I was sitting in my house with my kids in safety, feeling the warmth, trying to live normally.

'I want my kids to grow up and be good, find a job and start their life. However, this seems to be an almost impossible wish.'

Najah needs more corrective surgery to her jaw. 'I am not happy because it will cost the family a lot of money. I do not want my family to suffer any more,' she continued. 'I can take the pain but I will not inflict any more trouble on my kids. My treatment would take a long time and it would not be in Gaza, it has to be in Egypt or Jordan.

'I was never a political person. I do not feel shy or ashamed to say that all I cared for in life was my kids. I did not even understand politics. I never wanted anyone to suffer, even Israelis. Sadly I have changed my views: I am very angry at those criminals who devastated my life and my family. What have I done to deserve this? Now I wish the Israelis will suffer what we suffered; only then they will understand. Ahmad always says when he's deeply frustrated at the life he now has, "I hope that people who did this to my mother will have their mothers' hands amputated to feel the pain I feel."

'They cannot imagine the hatred they have created among us. This will last a long time.'

13

Death on Salahuddin Street

The car market has become a feature of east Gaza City, on the edge of Eastern Zaytoun. Every Saturday, hundreds will come from all over the Gaza Strip to buy and sell cars. The idea started with a few local car dealers meeting in an open area on the side of Salahuddin Street. Then it developed to become the largest car selling area in the Gaza Strip. Although it is beneficial for car merchants, buyers and sellers, it is unpleasant for travellers on Salahuddin Street. The car market expands out of the allocated yard to the main road, causing a lot of traffic jams.

Not far from the car market, towards Gaza City, is one of the famous landmarks in the Gaza Strip: the old Star drinks factory. Star is a fizzy orange drink: its factory used to be one of only two in the Gaza Strip. The other was Seven Up, which is also on Salahuddin Street, north of Gaza City. At the corner of the Star factory lies a cul-de-sac where Hashem Abu Ghali Hannouna received me.

'From the car market to here was like the Operation Command for the Israeli army during the land invasion,' Hashem said. 'I moved some of my kids away from the area to Tal Al Hawa, west of Gaza City, which was safer at the time. One of my daughters, Sabrin, her two toddlers and my 12-year-old son Ridwan stayed with us. For the previous four days there had been heavy shelling following the ground attack. Our area was under tank, F16 and Apache helicopter fire.

'Fifty people were hiding in our house; my brothers, some of our neighbours and their families. When the shelling intensified, I went with my wife Dalal, Ridwan, Sabrin and her two kids to my brother-in-law in the Al Rimal area. The rest of my kids went to hide in different relatives' houses.

'On 11 January 2009, we returned as I thought things had got calmer. We came back for a reason: there was no food in the shops and we had some food left in our house. We had flour as well, but no water, no electricity, nothing. We had a clay oven. My wife Dalal baked bread for everyone with a 20-kilo sack of flour; she was helpful and generous. She would regularly ask any passersby in our neighbourhood to come to our house for food or to have a cup of tea. The whole neighbourhood was very fond of her.

'Dalal told me, "It looks like normal over here." It was still during the truce declared by the Israeli army in the morning. For the previous four days they had declared a truce for four hours during the day. Before that there was none at all. She said, "Let's stay here and take our time getting more stuff for the people we're staying with." I agreed reluctantly to stay overnight at our house: I wish now I had not. We did not know this calm was for a reason. They were preparing for the night-time attack. At 9 p.m. there was no shelling, total calm. I was very happy; I prayed and thanked God. I used the water pump to fill the tanks. Dalal was happy too. She had a shower and put on brand new clothes; they were still in the packaging; all presents I had brought from Jordan. She also prayed. After that, we had supper during which the Israeli tanks and jet fighters started shelling the area. The sound was deafening.

'At approximately 11 p.m. a shell landed near our house. The tanks and the fighters were coming from the west. Minutes later, an F16 launched the attack on our house. It destroyed the front of our house; the kids were terrified. My granddaughter came to hide beneath my coat. My son's flat on top of our house was completely destroyed.

'Dalal went to my daughter's room to comfort her and the kids and keep them company. The F16 re-launched more attacks.

'I said to Dalal, "Let's leave through the fields nearby on the eastern side." We started to prepare to leave. I went to the toilet and two shells landed on the house. They destroyed the indoor lounge and the entrance to the house. I came out of the toilets, I could not see anything. Thick dust was everywhere. When the dust settled I found Dalal. She was kneeling as if she were praying. The left side of her face was completely missing. I saw she was already dead; I covered her. I took my son, daughter and her two kids out of the house. I still cannot remember how we got out. We walked for more than two kilometres; there was nobody in the streets until we came across a car which took us to my brother's house at Al Rimal.

'When I came back to collect Dalal's body the following morning, the tanks were only a little way down the street. With the help of my brothers we took the body out. The tanks started firing at us. We left the body in the street and hid for more than two hours. My sons, daughters, relatives and friends were waiting in Al Shifa hospital for the body to arrive.

'I appealed to many human rights organizations but no one could reach me. I phoned for ambulances but the answer was always the same: we cannot reach you; we are not allowed; it is too dangerous. They asked me to move her to Salahuddin Street. After two and a half hours the shooting stopped. We moved the body on a ladder.

'I regard myself as a patriot who loves his homeland but was never involved in politics. I worked for long years as a bus driver of the Israeli bus company, Eged. All I wanted was to be able to live a normal life, support my family and make them happy. I dealt with a lot of Israelis through my job in the past with no problem at all. I do not feel the same now after what we suffered. It is ironic that if you are a Palestinian death comes to you even if you are not interested in politics.

'We were married for 29 years. We had five boys and two girls. All of them are still suffering what seems to be long-lasting trauma; especially the younger ones. All of them have had psychological treatment since her death. Every day they pick up a photo of Dalal and start talking to her. Sometimes I join them; I always say to her, I wish it were me instead of you. They have nightmares all the time. They are not the same as before; they are not as happy. They always talk about death and remember what happened.'

Dalal's 16-year-old son Sa'ad sat with us remembering his mother with visible sadness. 'I was very mischievous when I was little. She would punish me but the punishment never lasted long. She had a big heart; always forgave me. My mother loved breeding birds and rabbits for her kids and grandchildren to play with.'

Dalal's brother Mohsen was listening despite the tears in his eyes. We had to stop many times to comfort him. 'I am nine years younger than Dalal,' Mohsen said. 'Dalal was very kind to me; I was born after four girls; I was their toy. We had a special relationship. During the olive harvest she always gave me olives and olive oil for my family, neighbours and friends. We remember her every olive season.'

'This, in my view, was a war crime: it was not an attack on Hamas. They wanted to punish everyone; it was a war against people. I am so happy with attempts to bring these criminals to justice. For me, I do not want revenge; justice is more important than revenge. I hope I will live until I see Olmert, Barak, Livny, Ashkenazi and other leaders who ordered this being brought to justice. I am disgusted at the stance of the Arab countries, as well as the American and European governments. No serious steps have been taken by any of these governments to bring justice to us.'

14

Hurry up and give me a needle and thread!

Mudallalah Joha sewed her children's clothes herself. This was her contribution to supporting her large family. She was a good seamstress; she did it with much pride. Even in her worst nightmares she did not expect to use her sewing skills in a way that would put her off sewing forever.

Mudallalah's family lives in Al Zaytoun Al Sharqi, east of Gaza. Her husband Mu'in is a retired agricultural engineer.

'Before the start of the land attack, the Israeli shelling of our district intensified,' Mu'in said. 'One garage was hit by a F16 rocket. The whole area shook violently. They also bombed a field in front of our house destroying 50-year-old olive trees. My brother said we should leave. We did not leave as our family is large, my mother is 85 years old, I have two disabled daughters, Momena and Fatima, I am diabetic and my wife, Mudallalah, suffers from breast cancer. It was not the right thing to do.

'The land attack started on 3 January 2009 at night. Fires in our area were breaking out for over six hours. The power was cut off. At about dawn they attacked our neighbours, the Al Hilou family home. Three were killed in that attack: Fouad, Muhammad and Farah. A 3-year-old child was also injured. The tanks started firing on our house. They hit the upper floor of our house directly. We felt the house shaking: the rubble was coming down on us. We all ran to hide in one room. My kids were screaming loudly; I felt utterly helpless. I asked them to start praying as we thought we would all die. Paratroopers landed on top of our house as they did on neighbouring houses.

'The Israeli army infantry came from the west side: they were firing intensely as if they were occupying a military post. My kids continued to scream loudly. I started crawling towards the lounge then returning. I did this many times; I did not know what I was doing.

'The soldiers ordered us to come downstairs. My 22-year-old daughter Samah was the bravest among all of us: she went down carrying a white flag. They fired over the top of her head and around her but luckily she was not injured. She screamed hysterically. They ordered us to get outside: men in front and the women behind. They ordered the men to strip above the waist and raise our hands up in the air.

'The house suffered a great deal of damage inside. One of the soldiers had a digital camera. He took photos of us and of the destruction, and he kept looking at us and laughing.

'My kids were crying. The officer in command told us they were going to destroy the house with explosives. I told the soldiers in Hebrew I have money and asked if I could take it. He refused. My wife's gold and money was stolen but we could not say anything. They said, "You will go to Rafah at the south of the Gaza Strip." They occupied the house after we left. They destroyed the furniture, the television, the computer. They threw the medical equipment for asthma and diabetes out of the windows. They even emptied the olive oil supplies for the year onto the floor. They made many holes at low levels in the walls of the upper floor for snipers to place their guns facing Salahuddin Street. The house was filthy when we came back. The Israeli soldiers defecated everywhere.

'One soldier rushed us; he pointed the gun at us and said, "Either you leave or will be shot," he said. We started moving south. We decided to go to the Abu Zour family who live not far from my house. They continued to fire over the top of our heads.

'We spent a night at Abu Zour's house. More than 45 people from the neighborhood were hiding there. With every rocket that landed nearby, we thought it was the end. The following morning, they fired intensively on the house from all directions. It felt like they wanted to finish us off: all of us. The external walls protected us but they were severely damaged. Then the soldiers stormed the house. They arrested my 18-year-old son Hatim and three other men and two children aged 14 from the Abu Zour family.'

Hatim recounted the terrifying events. 'They took us to an old house which they occupied. They forced us to strip naked. They beat us badly for one hour then they laughed and gave us 30 seconds head start to leave or be shot. I ran like mad until I rejoined my family.'

'My 14-year-old son Ibrahim saw the dead body of a child from the Hijji family at the side of the street. He shouted, "This is my classmate." He started crying loudly but Mudallalah said to keep moving. Another girl, Olla, from the Arafat family, was lying on the side of the road also bleeding but we could not help her. An Israeli sniper hit her with a bullet while she was moving on their orders.

'My mother fainted as a result of the arrest of my son Hatim, she loved him very much,' Mu'in continued. 'I lost all my energy. My kids carried her and we decided to go to some other neighbours, the Al Moghraby family. They have a garage adjacent to their house. The house was very crowded. There were more than 80 people hiding inside; more than six families. We decided to go somewhere else as there was no room for us.

'We moved my mother on a wheelbarrow borrowed from the Al Moghraby family. We went down Salahuddin Street towards the centre of Gaza City. We thought they would not attack us since we were waving white flags. Ibrahim was carrying a white flag with both hands. It was 5 January 2009 at approximately 1 p.m. The Israeli soldiers started firing on us. The first wave of bullets hit the pavement in front of me and my mother. A bullet hit Ibrahim in the chest. My sons and daughters screamed, "They killed Ibrahim, Daddy!" Muhammad started shouting. The sniper looked at him and laughed. He also pointed the gun at me and carried on laughing.

'My sons carried their brother and moved him back to the Al Moghraby house. He was awake and he told us "I am OK, do not worry. It is just a small injury in my chest." Blood was coming out of four holes in his chest. The bullet disintegrated inside him. The area had been declared a military zone by the Israeli army. Ambulances were prevented from reaching us.

'Mudallalah asked for a needle and thread, and cologne. She stitched up Ibrahim's wounds. For minutes he stopped bleeding but after that it continued to come out between the stitches. We kept phoning the local radio stations, the hospitals and the Red Cross but to no avail.'

'I held my brother while Mum was trying to stitch his wounds up,' Muhammad remembered. 'He felt nothing. He was still conscious, he kept saying, "I am thirsty, I am hungry." He was bleeding heavily. Mum told me he continued to bleed until he died at about 2 a.m. in the morning. Eleven hours bleeding, then dying without any proper medical help.'

'Had the ambulances been allowed to reach Ibrahim, he may have survived,' Mudallalah said, her voice full of sorrow. 'All the time he was saying his last prayers. His voice was getting weaker as time went by. He was very cold. His last moments were very emotional: he was lying at peace in my lap, unconscious, then he stopped breathing. I realized he had died. I was devastated. I kept his death from his father, his brothers and sisters until the following morning. I did not want to wake them up. I still do not know how I managed to stop myself screaming when Ibrahim died in my arms. But I guess when you are in the middle of a situation it is different from when you think back.'

Mu'in said, 'From Monday to Thursday we stayed at the Al Moghraby family home. We put Ibrahim's body outside during the day, hoping the Red Cross, or the Red Crescent, would pass by and take him but they could not reach the area. Muhammad heard the sirens many times but then the sound of machine guns firing.

'We slept in the cars in the garage as there was no space inside the house. It was extremely cold as it was January. We asked Abu Nabil Al Moghraby to move us to the lounge. Hours later an Apache attacked the garage: we were so lucky not to be there. Ibrahim's body was still in the garage but it was protected by one of the destroyed cars.'

'He was very kind to me,' Mudallalah said. 'Once he cut his hand trying to make a lamp for me on Mother's Day. He was very quiet;

he was shy. He concentrated on his studies. It has been two years since Ibrahim was taken away from me but to me the pain is still the same.'

Ibrahim's 14-year-old brother Yousif remembers him all the time. 'I miss him so much: I can never get the image of him bleeding and suffering during his last hours out of my mind. I keep having nightmares; I do not sleep as well as I used to do. We used to play football after school; Ibrahim loved football.'

'He used to love to sleep near me,' Mu'in said, pointing at his bed. 'He was so brave. He was funny. He used to do strange things to make his brothers and sisters laugh. Once he dressed himself up as a bride on her wedding day. He asked one of his brothers to dress up as a bridegroom. He sometimes slept on the window sill. His brothers and sisters found this very strange but funny at the same time.

'We always think death will come to us: we feel they denied us our future. The future looks bleak. My children are always scared. The war is over but our lives will never be the same.'

15

The baby is gorgeous, don't you think?

The tragedy of the Al Samouny family from Eastern Zaytoun has been recorded by the Goldstone Commission and by various human rights groups, as well as most of the journalists who covered the attacks on Gaza. This is why I was reluctant when Tamam Al Hindi of the National Society for Rehabilitation suggested I visit the two children from the Al Samouny family who are now disabled as a result of the attack. After all, I wanted this book to cover cases that did not have a lot of media attention.

Tamam had already phoned Wael, the father, to inform him we were going to visit. She phoned again to apologize. Wael was upset: he told her he had kept Abdullah and Muhammad off school especially to meet us. Tamam was persuasively insistent we should go if only to have a cup of coffee and say hello: I accepted. Afterwards, I realized what a terrible mistake it would have been not to have met Abdullah and Muhammad.

The road to the Al Samouny compound, in a farming area on the outskirts of Gaza off Salahuddin Street, still carries signs of the Israeli attack that destroyed virtually everything standing in that area.

Outside their house, which witnessed the full scale of the tragedy, we were met by Wael and his two sons, Abdullah, who is now 9, and 7-year-old Muhammad. They were severely disabled by the attack. Their brother Faris (13) and sister Rizqa (14) were killed.

The two boys were pleasant and charming, smiling throughout our meeting. Despite this you can feel a sense of sadness and detachment in Abdullah. It is no surprise after what he has witnessed. He spent four days in the same room as 22 dead people.

'On 4 January 2009 nearly a hundred members of our extended Samouny family were rounded up by the Israeli army,' Wael remembered. 'We were searched, some handcuffed and forced into my house. After an excruciating night crammed into the storeroom, the Israeli military started shelling the house. Twenty-one members of our family were killed as a result; of those, 10 were children and seven women. The youngest was my nephew, Muhammad Helmi Samouny, aged six months. Eight others were killed by Israeli forces in the same vicinity in two days.

'We decided to flee. The stronger ones among us carried as many of the wounded as we could. The women waved their scarves. Some family members were still alive but we had to leave them behind; it was agonizingly painful but we could not carry them.'

'My father carried me,' Abdullah interrupted. 'I told him, "Dad, leave me I am dying. Take my other brothers and sisters."'

'I left him for dead,' Wael continued. 'After proceeding a short distance down the road Israeli soldiers fired at us and ordered us to stop. "Go back or you will die," the soldiers shouted from a building they were occupying; they spoke in classical Arabic, not slang. We defied the orders of the soldiers and they continued to shoot at our feet. After walking for two kilometres along Salahuddin Street, we found ambulances to take the injured among us to the hospital.'

For the next four days, the Palestinian Red Crescent Society (PRCS), the International Committee for the Red Cross (ICRC) personnel and the Samounys themselves were prevented from reaching the compound to retrieve the dead, and rescue the injured left behind, including Abdullah. After the initial shelling, Israeli forces knocked down what remained of the houses with tanks or bulldozers.

The Israeli military finally allowed the ambulances to pass through. Incredibly, rescue workers found two children alive in the rubble of Wael Samouny's house, along with the bodies. One of the surviving children was 7-year-old Abdullah. It was another 13 days before all the bodies were recovered from the area.

'If the ambulances had been able to get through immediately after the attack or even on the second or the third day, there would have been more survivors,' Wael said. 'After everything that happened, we still want to know why: we are civilians.'

'I was inside the house for four days after the first attack,' Abdullah told me. 'I saw my brother, sister and grandmother among the dead; I saw all of them.

The smell from the dead bodies started to get stronger by the hour: it was terrible. We could not even think of trying to escape because we were severely injured.

'Images from the three horrific days keep coming back to haunt me. Every night I remember the dead: I dream of them. I wake up very scared, drink some water and go back to sleep.

'I heard ambulance sirens many times followed by waves of gunfire. The Israeli army shot at them whenever they tried to reach us. I thought everyone inside the house would die. The Israeli soldiers were very close to us. I was terrified they would come back and finish us off.

'I always hoped my parents would come back and take me. They later told me they tried hard to reach us but they were shot at every time they approached the area. I was covered in blood. The 22 martyrs were around me, I was sleeping on parts of their bodies. It was very scary at night-time.

'Some of the martyrs did not die straight away, they were in severe pain. Two of my cousins, Huda, who was shot in the eye, and Ishaq, died on the third day. During these three days they did not say anything just moaned quietly. Their mothers, Hanan and Om Ishaq, died in the same attack.

'My cousin Ahmad crawled to bring tomatoes to feed me as I could not move at all: this is how we survived during the four days: on tomatoes. My injury was filthy, the smell was intolerable: even the doctor at the hospital could not take it. When the Red Cross rescued me I was still conscious. I was the only one carried on a stretcher; the other injured were carried on carts and donkeys. The ambulances were still prevented from reaching us. They were parked near the car auction on Salahuddin Street.

'During the four days I was crying almost all the time. I was in severe pain. I could not sleep at all; this intensified my pain. Ahmad also carried me to go to the toilet. The house had still not been demolished. After the Red Cross collected us, they destroyed the house on top of the dead bodies of the 22 martyrs.

'I love all my brothers and sisters. I hoped I would be able to see them again but I didn't think I would. Despite everything, I am extremely happy to be back with my parents, brothers and sisters: the most painful part of my experience was when I saw my brother, sister and grandmother killed in front of me.

'My teachers used to consider me to be one of the good pupils at school: not any more. I just cannot concentrate. They understand. When I am in the classroom I always remember what happened. I cannot get the picture of my brother, sister, grandmother and others around me out of my head.

'After they rescued me from the house, I could not talk for six days. I could not eat or sleep properly. I am still receiving psychological treatment two years later.

'I stopped playing sport for a long time but now I am back playing a little bit. Playing makes me forget for a while. I am delighted my mother gave birth to a new baby: we called him Faris after my dead brother. I always play with him; he gives me loads and loads of happiness. When I am with him I forget completely what happened to me.'

Abdullah asked Muhammad and their sister Suzanne to bring Faris for me to see. The baby was sleeping in his cot. 'He is so gorgeous, don't you think so?' Abdullah said, with a wide smile.

In the middle of telling me about his horrific experience Abdullah wanted to show me the severity of his injury. He tried to take his jumper off but he could not. He still cannot move his shoulder upwards. Muhammad rushed to help. I saw how committed he is to his brother, despite his obvious emotion.

It was then Muhammad's turn to tell me his story. 'My hand was bleeding heavily from my elbow. My father was also bleeding from his injuries. I was crying all the time, the pain was too much to tolerate. At the hospital, they put me on one bed and my father on another. I was told later that due to the circumstances and the facilities the operation was not successful. I need another operation to correct my elbow. I am hoping I will be able to leave the Gaza Strip to have my operation.'

Their sister Suzanne, a beautiful 11 year old with one of the most charming smiles I have ever seen, kept hugging Abdullah and

Muhammad throughout our interview. 'I thought Abdullah was dead. We used to sit together to watch cartoons. *Tom and Jerry* is our favourite cartoon. We would pretend one of us was Tom and the other was Jerry.' Muhammad and Abdullah laughed. 'We always fought about who would be the mouse: Muhammad always wanted to be the mouse because he is cleverer than the cat. These were the loveliest memories. We try to do this again now but we do not get the same feeling of happiness. I feel sadder than before. I was always happy, now I always remember my brother and sister and what happened. I always want revenge.'

'I hope the people who launched the rockets on our family will be punished for what they did to us,' Abdullah sighed. 'I will never be the same. Before the war I saw life as beautiful; I was very active. Now I feel like crying all the time. I do this regularly.

'I hope one day I will be normal again; as normal as any other child in the world. At the moment I find it difficult to cope, but one day I am sure I will be able to. The love and care of my family, friends and people all over the world whom I do not even know nor have ever met will no doubt help me through.'

Just before I left Abdullah asked me to take a photo of him and Faris. Suzanne and Muhammad joined him; they were all happy around their little baby brother.

Abdullah said while seeing me out, 'These are the best moments of my life when I am with little Faris.'

16

I will be part of the farewell ship

I drove away from the Al Samouny family home southwards on Salahuddin Street to Al Qarrara village, not far south of Gaza City. I was on my way to meet my relatives, Adel and his wife, the parents of Izz ad-Din El-Farra, a 13-year-old child who was killed during the attacks.

I passed by the Abu Holy area which is on the edge of their village. It is shocking how the landscape of this area has changed since 2000. For someone like me who knew it well it is difficult to understand this deterioration. This used to be one of the most beautiful landscapes in the Gaza Strip. Orange and guava orchards, olive groves and vineyards covered most of it.

My father spent long periods working hard on developing this land. He paid out a sizeable part of his salary and my mother's salary on it. We did not make much money from it. As a youngster I always wondered what was the point of having this land and not getting any income from it. The Israelis exploited us, as they did all people who owned agricultural land or were farmers. I remember we sold one tonne of oranges for 35 Jordanian dinars; the equivalent of 25 pounds at the time. At the end of the season there was always a loss, but my father was always happy. His philosophy was different from ours. He always told us keeping this land green and fertile is an important form of resistance to the Israeli occupation. Nothing hurts them more than to see us successful in any way – and land is a key part of this, he always said: I did not appreciate this at the time, but I came to respect it greatly as I grew older.

One of the most joyous times of my father's life was in the early seventies when we struck water for the first time. My mother Laila was over the moon: water means life and now we had our own well, we did not have to rely on buying it from neighbouring suppliers. My mother cooked a massive meal; all our neighbours and relatives from Al Qarrara village came to celebrate with us. It is a common cultural practice in the Gaza Strip to invite people for a feast whenever water is discovered. Our well became a local landmark with its high masonry tower providing a water head to push water down to irrigate the orange and olive trees. My father cupped water in his hands and asked my sister Mona, my brother Mones and I to drink from his hands. This was a symbolic and moving moment for him.

Unfortunately, due to our different circumstances, none of us was able to keep the land as well looked after as my father did. One of the most emotional times in my family history took place after the passing away of my father. My mother always asked to be taken to the Abu Holy land, as she called it. 'Take me there, I can see your father's face in every orange tree.'

In November 2000, the phone rang in my house in Rotherham, South Yorkshire. On the other end was my sister Mona. In a shaky voice she said, 'I have bad news: the Israeli army has razed our entire land in Abu Holy, together with our house and well.' I naively asked, 'What about the Jummaiz trees and the red berry tree?'[21] 'Everything,' Mona said. They destroyed our family house, the well and land together with hundreds of donoms of the most fruitful land in the neighbourhood in a matter of a day or two; as well as memories of the most fantastic times of our lives, and priceless family photographs from the thirties and the forties of the last century.

---

[21] It was a common myth in the Gaza Strip at the time that Jummaiz trees were the cause of the many invasions the area suffered, including the British Mandate. Many people seriously believed the occupying powers wanted to occupy the Gaza Strip partly because they had heard of a tree that gives fruit six times a year. This tree was the Jummaiz. Of course this was not true, but it was part of people's talk in the sixties and early seventies.

I suppose we were the lucky ones in this awful situation. At least my family had another house in the town. Others had nowhere to go following the demolition of dozens of houses in the same army operation. Some went to stay with relatives; others stayed in tents provided by the Red Cross. These people have lived on their land for centuries. They have been known individually by the Israeli army for over three decades since the settlements were built. They have not been involved in any anti-Israeli acts of resistance. Yet all this was not enough reason to spare them the severe suffering and loss of livelihood imposed on them. It was simply a collective punishment to teach others who dared to resist the Israeli occupation a lesson.

I tried to comfort Mona but without success. This was our childhood being destroyed. That red berry tree was the most painful to lose. To us it was more than a tree. It carried memories of my mother Laila cooking the most fantastic food every spring and summer weekend. We would gather, sometimes with friends or relatives, to have our dinner under the tree, then stay talking and socializing late into the evening before going back to our house in Khan Younis. When my father passed away, and the land was divided between us, all of us wished the red berry tree to be on our share of the land. Mones was the lucky one. Mona asked him in front of us all, in a voice taut with emotion, 'Mones, please promise us to keep the tree no matter what.' Naturally, he promised.

My mother was the most devastated. She refused to go and see the damage: she could not believe it and did not want to face the reality of the situation. She would turn her face away from the land whenever we passed it on our way to Gaza and back. It was extremely difficult for her to bear.

One of the memories indelibly etched in my mind is when my father wanted to kick fear out of us. He used the orange grove to do so. He would pick a pitch-black night and take my brother and I to the orange grove. He would promise us a reward if we would bring him something hidden in a tree at the very end of the grove. Mones would go first: after a while he would come back victorious with the sweet in his hand. I would then follow and do the same: it was initially terrifying but gradually we felt comfortable and less scared. My mother was not keen on this at all. She always tried to stop us without success. 'What is the point? Let them grow older and then they will naturally not be scared of things,' she would say but my father insisted.

I made a big mistake: I told my two young sons, Qasem and Qayis, this story. They were impressed and started asking me, 'When will we go to that orange grove? I want you to do to us what Jiddo [Granddad] Qasem used to do to you.' I feel terrible about this: how can I make this happen with the orange grove long gone?

My mother always cried when she remembered one cherished story. I was visiting home in 1990 and it was the first time my family met my six-month-old daughter Dana. My father took us all to the orange grove. He picked an orange, put it in Dana's hand and told her, 'Here it is Dana; your orange from your grove.' Obviously, Dana does not remember her visit but what my father said will remain in my family's memory as one of our sweetest memories of him.

This orange grove was part of our extended family history. My nephews and nieces, Nadia, Nael, Nuha, Muhammad and Basma, went there with my father. They loved to swim in the irrigation channels and my father used to sing them all kinds of songs; sometimes naughty ones to the dismay of my serious mother. After all, she was a headteacher for 25 years and in her book children must not be naughty, not even slightly. All her appeals to my father fell on deaf ears and the children continued to enjoy themselves with him.

In the late seventies I once asked my sister Maha's three-year-old twins Nael and Nuha to chant anti-occupation slogans when the Israeli infantry soldiers were about to pass by the orange grove. I told them that if they did it I would give them a chocolate bar each. When the soldiers passed both of them started chanting enthusiastically. The soldiers aggressively told them off. Immediately after that Nael came to me asking, 'Where is my chocolate?' at which I laughed a lot. After all, to a child the chocolate bar was the driving force behind his patriotic act. I suppose one might think this was a blatant use of children for political reasons. However, in Palestine children are fed attitudes that are anti-occupation with their mother's milk. When you are denied the basic human rights other people take for granted politics become your family's daily bread.

Dozens of chickens from our neighbour's land used to come to our orange grove every day causing much damage to the soil irrigation channels. My brother Mones eventually got fed up. He decided to punish them. Mones and his friend Wdaid caught a chicken, slaughtered it and cooked it for us. The following day a woman came asking for the chicken. She had counted her chickens and one was missing; she was adamant the chicken was in our orange grove when it disappeared. To our shock, Mones admitted he took it but then dropped a hilarious bombshell. 'I thought that it was a wild chicken,' he said. The place erupted into laughter, including the woman herself. No one had ever heard of a wild chicken. The woman carried on laughing and did not ask for any compensation.

My father was a tough self-made person who had to leave school when he was only 9 years old to help support his family after the death of my grandfather, Hussain, at a young age. This was to the disappointment of his teachers who saw him as a bright and promising pupil. My father and his older brother Abdulsallam had to work to help support their mother Muftiah, little brother Muhammad and sister Ruqaiyah. They all experienced childhood poverty unlike us. My father and Uncle Abdulsallam moved to Yaffa, or Jaffa as it is known in English, to work. They worked in different fields to support the family. My uncle Muhammad went to the USA where he finished his doctorate in international law. He returned to become an ambassador for Syria and Jordan at the UN where he became the president of the UN Security Council for one of its sessions. He was one of the top Arab diplomats of his generation and ended his professional life as the Under Secretary of the Arab League. My father went back to Khan Younis to become the director of the local council and later a member of the first Palestinian Legislative Council in the 1960s. Uncle Abdulsallam continued to live in Yaffa until the 1948 Nakba, when he was forced to leave his house and work and come back to Khan Younis. My father chartered a boat in the middle of the war to help Uncle Abdul Salam flee Yaffa with his wife Alia and their 7-year-old daughter Saheer under fire. They both told us how terrifying this experience was.

The Abu Holy area used to be in the middle of Gush Qatif, the biggest settlement block in the Gaza Strip.[22] In November 2000, after the start of the second *Intifada*, the Israeli army razed hundreds of donoms of this area destroying groves, wells and property. The 80-donom guava orchard, which belonged to our neighbours, the Abu Holy family, who relied on it to survive, was uprooted completely. In a matter of hours this family lost an annual income of approximately 18,000 pounds.

The excuse? For security reasons; to give their occupation army and settlers the freedom of movement. It was also in the middle of the Abu Holy area that the Israeli army established their largest checkpoint in the Gaza Strip.

For nearly six years thousands of Palestinians had to wait for long hours on both sides of the checkpoint to cross.

Lucky people went through in 90 minutes; others who were not so lucky waited for four hours. The truly unlucky ones waited for 12 hours or more. On many occasions hundreds of people had to sleep overnight on both sides of the checkpoint.

Many students from southern towns and villages missed their first two lectures on a daily basis. Frequently they missed the whole day.

---

[22] Israeli settlements were built on Palestinian land confiscated by Israel in the Gaza Strip. They have occupied, together with Israeli army military bases, 40 per cent of the land of the Gaza Strip for nearly four decades since 1967. The settlements were built on the most fertile land of the area. The settlement block of Gush Qatif was constructed on top of the largest underground water aquifer in the Gaza Strip. Only a maximum of 6,000 Jewish settlers lived in these settlements while over 1.5 million Palestinians were crammed into the remaining 60 per cent: a very small strip of land.

The Israeli army imposed a curfew on the Gaza Strip from 6 p.m. to 6 a.m. every night for the entire duration of the first Palestinian uprising (*Intifada*) from December 1987 to September 1993. This was on top of full days of curfew. During the first Gulf war in 1991 Israel imposed a 57-day curfew on the Gaza Strip.

As a result Al Azhar and Islamic universities had to open classes in Khan Younis (the second biggest city in the Gaza Strip, six kilometres to the south of the Abu Holy checkpoint) to allow students to attend lectures. Ambulances carrying patients to and from the southern area were also often stopped for hours. One might ask why would people not go home if the checkpoint was closed for hours? It's a logical thing to say but the Israeli army regularly shot at people who tried to leave the queue.

The closure was always without notice, reason or explanation. At other times Palestinians would wait in the heat of the summer or the winter cold for hours, only to watch one or two settler cars pass from one settlement to the other.

Many pregnant women gave birth in the most trying of circumstances at the Abu Holy checkpoint as well as at many other West Bank checkpoints. It was most difficult when the Abu Holy checkpoint was closed for days or even weeks. This simply meant people from the north of the Gaza Strip who were visiting the south, or vice versa, would be stuck for long periods. Some of them had relatives to stay with, others would stay at mosques nearby. Many weddings had to be postponed as the bride and the groom could not reach the wedding hall which happened to be on the wrong side of the checkpoint. Many of my relatives and friends could not attend my own wedding in 2001 as they were worried about not being able to get home the same evening.

The removal of this checkpoint, following the redeployment of the Israeli troops from the Gaza Strip to the Border, gave a real feeling of freedom to Palestinians there. It took many people a long time to believe the situation had changed; that they could travel from Khan Younis to Gaza, for example, in 20 minutes rather than 12 hours.

In 2004, on a visit to the Gaza Strip, I was on my way in a taxi from Khan Younis to Gaza when we were stopped at the Abu Holy checkpoint. The soldiers ordered the taxi driver to drive into an area surrounded by high concrete walls. They ordered us out of the car while pointing guns at us. I realized after a while we were standing on what used to be our orange grove. The area had changed so much it was difficult even for someone like me to recognize it straightaway.

Kassab (second from the right) celebrating with his local team

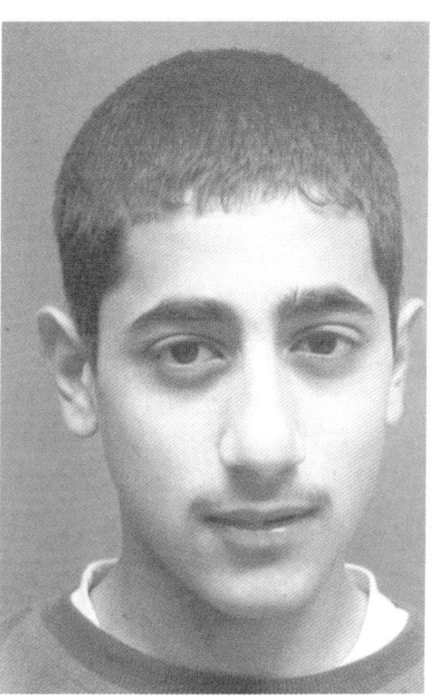

Ibrahim Abu Daqa

Kassab's graduation project

Islam with her mother and her brother Ahmad

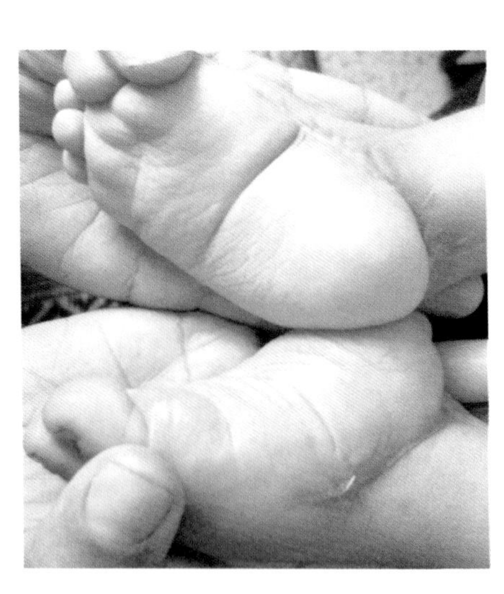

One of Islam's many operations

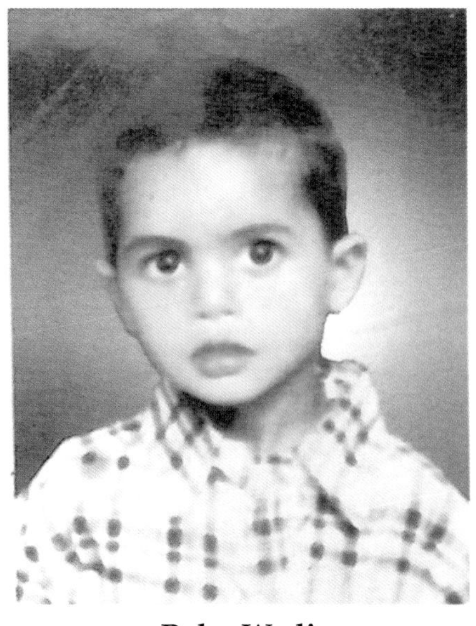

Baha Wadi, 7 years old

Muhammad Totah training for the black belt

Muhammad after the incident

Najah after losing her right arm and Ahmad with his work tools

Hashem with the portrait of Dalal,
his late wife

Graffiti left by Israeli soldiers
(photo by Eva Bartlett)

Part of the damage to the Joha family's house

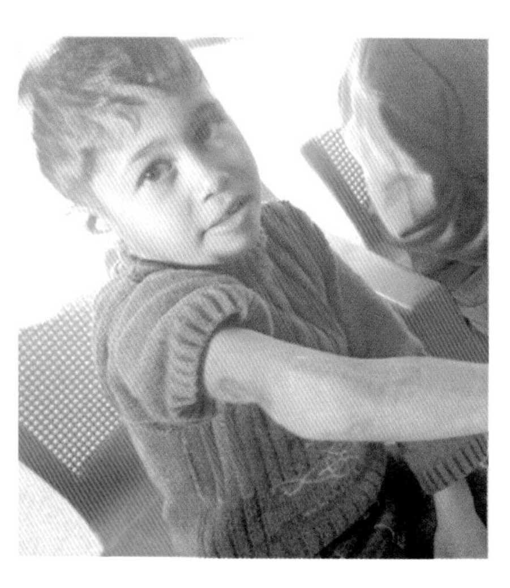

Muhammad Al Samouny showing his injury

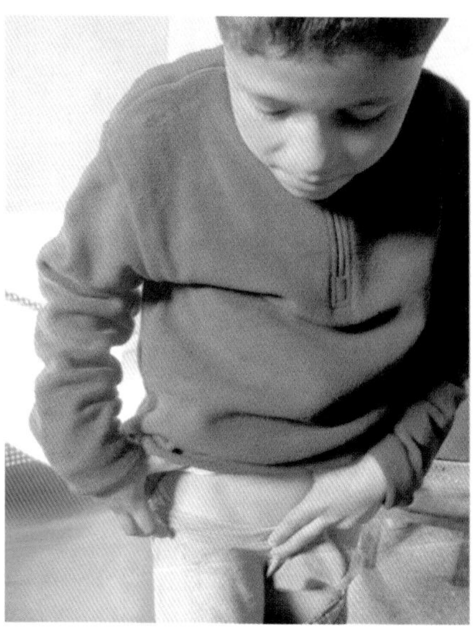

Abdullah showing his leg injury

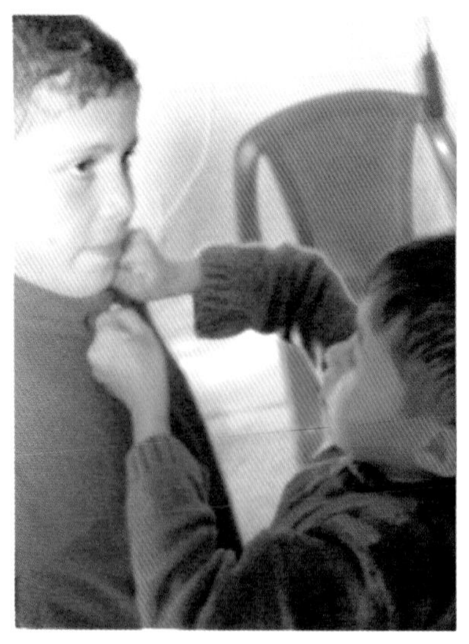

Muhammad helping Abdullah undress to show his shoulder injury

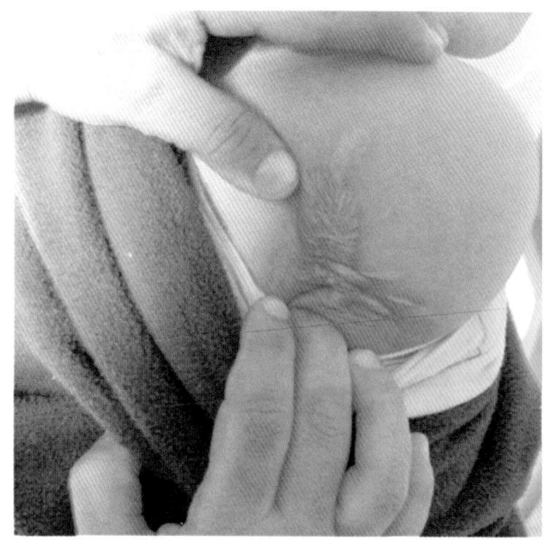

Abdullah's shoulder injury

Abdullah, Muhammad and Suzanne with their baby brother Faris

Izzeldin receiving a medal at school

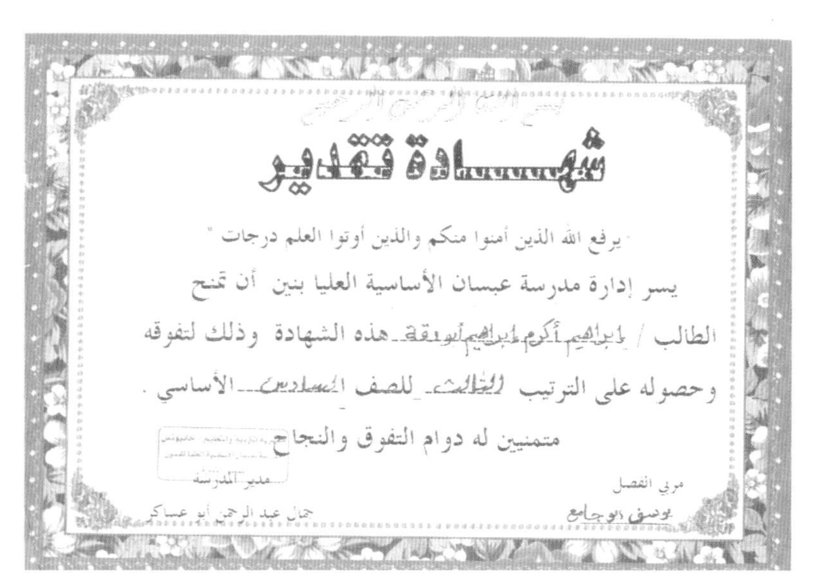

شهادة تقدير

" يرفع الله الذين أمنوا منكم والذين أوتوا العلم درجات "

يسر إدارة مدرسة عبسان الأساسية العليا بنين أن تمنح

الطالب / ابراهيم أكرم ابراهيم [illegible] هذه الشهادة وذلك لتفوقه

وحصوله على الترتيب الثالث للصف السادس الأساسي .

متمنين له دوام التفوق والنجاح

مربي الفصل | مدير المدرسة

يوسف ابو جامع | جمال عبد الرحمن أبو عساكر

Ibrahim Shurab's certificate of achievement

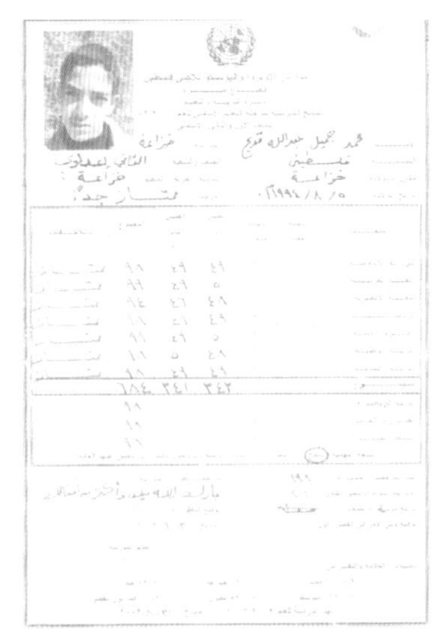

Muhammad's school certificate, of which the family is very proud

Aziza Abu Rouk with the photo of her son Abdullah

After a few hours and much interrogation they ordered us back and we continued to Gaza. I spent five weeks in Gaza during that visit. I travelled between my town Khan Younis and Gaza City almost every day. I had to go through the checkpoint every time. Time after time it got more and more upsetting, humiliating and infuriating. After queuing for hours every day I started to think what if I had to do this all year round or for several years, as the rest of my fellow Gazans have to. How would I react? After all, it is my homeland, my own country, and I am stopped even from moving freely. Would I react violently by whatever means possible, as have many Palestinians? I did not know the answer then. I still do not know it now.

I arrived at my relative Izzeldin's house and his father Adel received us warmly. Sheikh Adel, as he has been known locally for years due to his religious affiliation and his long beard, is a distant cousin and a friend of mine. It was very moving as we had not met for years. We were both students at Egyptian universities back in the late seventies. We sat down, exchanging university memories, then precious childhood ones of Al Qarrara village. Then, we played with other friends all over the place, swam in the irrigation pools and went to eat at a friend or relative's house. Adel was always sociable, friendly and humorous; nothing has changed despite his cruel loss.

Close to Adel's house, when a young teenager, I attended many pre-wedding celebrations, famously known as *Samir*. Men and women gather in two adjacent areas for many nights prior to the wedding night to socialize and dance. We stand shoulder to shoulder, led by a lead dancer who sings as well. The songs are Bedouin melodies which praise the bride, the groom and their families in an exaggerated yet charming way.

The *Samir* will last for hours every night. The most exciting part of the dance is when a woman appears brandishing a sword. We all pretend to be very excited: the rhythm of the dance increases; the singing gets faster; and we move forward towards the woman, out of excitement about her beauty, until we are very close to her. She waves the sword in our faces and we retreat, then try again and again to no avail: we never get her. This act goes on for a long time with different men and women taking part. The *Samir* also used to be a chance for local popular poets to show off their talent. The spontaneity of these poets was unbelievable. Two of them would stand in front of each other: one would start praising himself, his family and neighbourhood and cleverly belittle the other poet. The other would respond, and this goes on and on. In the process impressive and spontaneous popular poetry would be created.

One of the most embarrassing yet funniest memories of my youth (of which I am not proud) happened at Al Qarrara. Sheikh Muhammad El Saqqa, who was married to my father's aunt, was one of the main leaders of the Sufi movement in the Gaza Strip. He lived just south of Adel's house in Al Qarrara. Sufis are a peaceful religious group. They dedicate their lives to God. Sheikh Muhammad's son, Abdul Rahman, was working as a civil engineer in Kuwait at that time. Every time he came back to visit family the followers of his late father, known locally as 'Darawish', would come and ask him to have an evening to remember their leader Sheikh Muhammad. Abdul Al Rahman would slaughter many sheep and invite all the Darawish and plenty of others to a feast in remembrance of his father. My father always got invited to this event. Once he asked me, Mones and a relative, Wdaid, to go with him; a decision he lived to regret.

After we had eaten, we joined the Darawish in a circle and started to follow their movements, repeating their words of praise to God. Initially it was a slow and relaxing movement which was extremely soothing. Eventually, as they got more spiritual, they moved faster and faster and they became frenzied. Their words of praise turned into speedily mumbled noises. Their faces looked as if they were really in a different higher medium. At this stage, Wdaid fell on the floor laughing uncontrollably and Mones followed him; I tried to resist laughing but was not able to. Three of us were flat on the floor laughing hysterically. The leader of the Darawish approached us and angrily shouted, 'Laugh now, you will burn in hell in future!' My father was so angry; he kicked us out and never invited us again.

Reluctantly, I left the happy past for the reality of the present. I composed myself to hear their important account. Adel's wife, Om Bilal, remembered the day when Izz was killed. She showed visible strength which was, to put it moderately, very endearing. 'It was Wednesday: Izz, as we used to call him, went down to his uncle's house. He brought some logs for me to burn. He also helped his cousin Khadija to bake biscuits until sunset, at approximately 5 p.m. He then went out with his 15-year-old cousin Abdul Ghani on their bicycles to buy groceries from the shop nearby, only 300 metres away from our house.

'I heard a massive explosion; I did not know what had happened. I heard the sirens of the ambulances in our street. I checked on the kids to see who was missing. They told me Izz had not come back yet from the grocery shop. I felt there was something wrong; I felt as a mother that it was Izz whom the ambulances came for. I cannot explain to you why but that is how I felt. I had had a bad nightmare a few days before that a plane hit him; it swung left then right, then it hit him. You may find this strange but this is what happened. We then had a phone call from the hospital. It was a relative, confirming that Izz had been hit by a rocket from an Israeli drone. He died instantly. His cousin Abdul Ghani was seriously injured. He is still disabled in both legs.

'We used to get out a lot during the war. Our area was a quiet one, no rockets were launched from here. This was during the last few days of the attack on the Gaza Strip.

'Three days before he was killed, the kids were playing, they were happy. I was very happy to see them happy. I looked at them and wondered: will this happiness last? It was not meant to be.

'Izz was my companion, he went with me everywhere. He was the youngest of my children. In our culture, I guess as anywhere else in the world, the youngest is always special. He had a very nice voice; he was a member of the mosque *Inshad* team [choir] and also at school.

'His schoolmates and teachers were devastated. The school held a special tribute for him. They invited us; it was very emotional. They spoke about how popular he was. He won a lot of prizes for achievement at school. I have never cried in my entire life as much as I did at the tribute. The headteacher broke down in tears during his speech; he struggled a lot to complete it. One of his classmates also could not finish his speech. The headteacher put up so many posters of Izz around the school. He favoured him a lot because he was very well-mannered and well-disciplined.

'Izz loved to play with young kids. He had a very special relationship with his 4-year-old niece Raghd. When he was killed, she cried a lot. A few days ago she saw one of his photos, she hugged it and cried. She keeps imagining Izz is still alive.

'He always looked after our goats; they were his favourite animals. He always thought of himself as older than his age. Even when I gave him money, he looked after it, spending it carefully.

'He was a good sportsman, especially football. He was a member of the school team. He always came to me after matches with different schools to tell me all about the match. He won many medals with the team.

'He wanted to be an English language teacher. He was always trying to improve his English. This gave him an edge over his classmates.

'Something really strange happened a few days before his murder by the Israeli army. He kept singing two songs: 'I will be part of the farewell ship' and 'Farewell Farewell Farewell'. I never asked him why he sang these: I regret that now.

'His cousins are still grief-stricken: Reem (11) is the worst affected. She keeps seeing Izz in frequent nightmares. This affects her deeply. She is getting better and we all hope she will be back to normal.

'We were once at a party and the organizers wanted Izz to play the role of the martyr. He was shy but we encouraged him; he played the role very competently. He did not move at all; the mother of the martyr in the play was screaming but he did not move. I got worried, I thought something had happened to him. I went on stage to check, I hugged him and he opened his eyes and said, "Mum, don't embarrass me, I am only acting! Go back to your seat." Everyone in the hall laughed but I had to make sure after his persuasive performance.'

Om Bilal does not hide her affiliation to Hamas. 'Yes, we do support Hamas; in fact Izz was named after Izzeldin Al Qassam.[23] However, was Izz a resistance fighter? I would have felt less pain if

---

[23] Izzeldin Al Qassam was

a Syrian [of] devout and cultured parentage, he went to Egypt and studied at Al-Azhar. On his return to Syria, Qassam became a military he were, but he was just a child. He was like a little rose full of dreams; they destroyed his dreams and ours. They took away his most basic human right which is to live. I think that in their considerations human rights are only applicable to Zionists.

'What really hurt me was the false rumours spread after the incident. They said Izz and Abdul Ghani were on their way to deliver a mobile phone to one of the resistance fighters from the al-Qassam Brigades, the military wing of Hamas. The mobile phone was intercepted by the Israeli army and this is why the drone launched the attack. Totally false: they can say what they like but we know the truth.'

(cont.) leader in one of the uprisings against French rule . . . The French sentenced him to death. He fled to Haifa in Palestine. There he taught, preached did charitable work and set up a night school for illiterates . . . Everywhere he warned of the gravity of the Zionist invasion. Verses from the Quran, particular those which called for struggle and sacrifice, were constantly on his lips.

Over the years, he gathered about himself . . . 800 followers. 200 of them received military training. They pledged to give their lives for Palestine. They were expected to supply their own arms and to contribute all else they could to the cause . . .

Qassam and a group of his closest comrades, almost all of them peasants, made their way inland to the wooded hills of Jenin. They had sold their wives' jewellery and some of their household furnishings to buy rifles and ammunition. They spent the daytime in caves, near the village of Ya'bud. At night they attacked the Zionists. The British . . . sent its forces aided by reconnaissance planes to hunt them down. Sheikh Izzeldin Qassam was forced into a premature battle. Called upon to surrender, he refused. He encouraged his followers to 'die as martyrs'. After a battle lasting several hours, Qassam and three or four companions were killed, the rest were captured. A huge throng attended his funeral in Haifa. He was buried ten kilometres away in the village of Yajou . . . It had been a brief and – from a military point of view – futile rebellion. But it stirred up the Palestinian masses; that was all Sheikh Qassam had hoped for. (David Hurst, *The Gun and Olive Branch* (London: Faber, 2003)).

'I feel very angry, they burnt my heart,' Om Bilal continued. 'I hope they will one day feel similar pain. Please write this in your book; I want the world to know how we feel.

'When I pass the spot he was killed I always become very sad. I recall the circumstances of his death. However, my faith gives me a lot of strength: after all, he is now a bird in Paradise. I always sympathized with people who lost loved ones: now I feel I am part of this group. I understand and feel their suffering a million times more.

'What the Israelis do not realize is that we are much more determined on resistance following their attacks. Even if they threaten us with nuclear power, they will not intimidate me. Yes, they are strong, and we are weak, but our will to continue until we liberate our land is a lot stronger, and will continue to be for long time.'

17

Grass for the goats

I left my family house in Khan Younis to go to the small town of Abasan Al Kabeera just to the east to meet the Abu Daqqa family – they lost two of their children, brothers Muhammad and Ibrahim.

As I entered Bani Suhaylah town to the east of Khan Younis I passed my old Al Bursh preparatory school. The school was named after its long serving headteacher, the late Muhammad Al Bursh (Abu Ibrahim), a man of great educational skills who enjoyed the trust of all inhabitants. It was very common in the Gaza Strip to name schools after headteachers, men and women. On the other side, after we passed Bani Suhaylah, I saw the road which leads to Al Awda Secondary School. This brought back a lot of memories from my secondary school days. It was at Al Awda that I played a few basketball matches against Al Awda team. On one occasion things got so heated that the supporters of Al Awda invaded the court and we had to run for safety. However, no grudges were held and the two school teams were friends again within days.

Akram Abu Daqqa stood outside his house at Abasan Al Kabeera waiting for me. A patient quiet man, he shows signs of being resigned to the tragedy that hit his household. His two sons, Ibrahim, 16, and Muhammad, 14, were killed during the attacks on the Gaza Strip.

'Ibrahim and Muhammad loved animals,' Akram said. 'One of the goats in our yard gave birth to two kids. They argued with their younger brother, 13-year-old Shady, about who would take the goats. They decided Muhammad would take one and Shady one. Their little sister Iman was not happy and started crying: she wanted a goat to herself. Muhammad promised her the next one would be hers. He fulfilled his promise despite protests from his other brothers and sisters. It was this love and care for their animals that made Ibrahim and Muhammad go to their cousin Hana's house to fetch grass to feed them.'

Akram continued, 'My niece Hana Abu Daqqa, who doesn't live far from here, asked for help to clear their yard. Ibrahim and Muhammad took advantage of the ceasefire declared by the Israeli army. They went on their bicycles to help her and they asked Hana if they could take some of the grass to our goats. Hana agreed. Muhammad and Ibrahim came home for a wheelbarrow and some bags, and then they went back to Hana's house in the early afternoon. They played for a bit with the other kids outside Hana's house. Then they walked towards the house. As they arrived at the door they were hit directly by an Israeli land-to-land missile. Their bodies were smashed into bits. Shady saw the whole thing. "They all died instantly," he told me. Parts of their flesh was splattered on the wall nearby. Ibrahim Abu Tayr, an elderly man in his sixties, collecting weeds on his land nearby was also killed in the same attack.

'The area where my niece lives is quiet and safe. Nobody had been killed in this area since the start of the war on 27 December 2008. It is an area known not to have any resistance activity even during the first and second *Intifada*. This is why we expected no trouble at all. There were no resistance fighters; it is at least four kilometres from the border.

'I believe the attack was deliberate: the army deliberately targeted my children. It was clear Muhammad and Ibrahim were civilians. The drone saw them clearly: the order must have been be deliberate.

'Muhammad was a student at Al Awda preparatory school, Ibrahim was a student at Al Mutanabi secondary school.'

Their mother Sabah joined us. 'I suffered a lot of pain; until now I go through long periods of not being able to sleep at all; I lost two sons, how I can forget them? It is impossible. They kept coming to me in my dreams: they told me they were not dead. I always hoped they would continue to appear in my dreams but they do not any more. I feel very sad about this. Sometimes I beat myself up, thinking they were upset with me when they died, and this is why they do not appear in my dreams anymore.

'Ibrahim always told me, "Sabah, I want to be a doctor to be able to help people." He was very committed to his study. He was serious, unlike Muhammad who was always joking and creating a funny atmosphere.

'He had big dreams. He was very generous; he would always give some of his pocket money to his poor schoolmates. He was very promising.

'Muhammad was a member of the school radio station. He used to prepare some material and read it on the school radio. Had I known I would lose them I would have recorded every breath in their life.

'Life has a different taste after them. They filled my life with joy and happiness.' Sabah started crying loudly and could not speak.

'Muhammad loved cats,' Shady remembered. 'He brought his first cat home from the street; it was very weak and ill. He called it Bassabis. He used to feed her himself; she would not accept food from anyone else. He looked after her with great interest and kindness. After he died she ran away, we looked for her everywhere but we could not find her.

Their 20-year-old brother Ahmad recounted with obvious sorrow, 'I used to go out with my two brothers; we used to play football together. They were both passionate about football. Muhammad loved to sing; he had a lovely voice. I miss my brothers too much.'

'It is evident whenever the Israeli army invades that they try to kill as many as they can, destroy the trees, the animals. If they lose one soldier they collectively punish the whole area: this is unfair. We think they want to finish us all. All the soldiers and their commanders are guilty. They hate us: even if we try not to hate them they force us to by their atrocities. They breed hatred within us from childhood,' Ahmad continued.

'Both Muhammad and Ibrahim had no political affiliation at all,' Akram interrupted. 'Of course, they respected anyone who resisted the occupation but they took no part in any paramilitary activity. Their lives were cut short for no reason but hatred.

'We had a baby after the war. Muhammad loved the name Qussai; this is why we called him Qussai.

Life goes on, but they are always in our minds. I always hoped they would grow up to be good members of society; all was destroyed.

'When I heard the British Government is planning to pass a law to stop the prosecution of Israeli war criminals, I felt very offended: why should they do that, I wonder. What happened to my two sons was a war crime. I do not care if they have lawyers who can spin the facts. We know the truth of what happened on that terrible day. Nothing has been done to achieve justice as yet. Many human rights organizations took our statements and photos of what happened but nothing has happened: we simply want justice.

'I would like to convey a message to the mothers of the soldiers who killed my sons in cold blood: "My sons had done nothing. Do you understand my pain? You do not. Unfortunately, you would not feel my pain until you suffer the same: this is the tragedy and the vicious circle which we live in." Our blood is so cheap to them; one soldier like Shalit is more important to the world than an entire people.'[24]

---

[24] Gilad Shalit is an Israeli corporal of the Israeli army captured inside Israel near the Kerem Shalom crossing by Izz ad-Din al-Qassam Brigades, Popular Resistance Committees, and Army of Islam in a cross-border raid via underground tunnels near the Israeli border with Gaza on 25 June 2006. Hamas held him for over five years, until his release on 18 October 2011 in a deal that secured the release of 1,027 Palestinian political prisoners.

18

No place like home

I left the Abu Daqqa family to travel east to visit the Qdaih family in Ikhza'a town. Ikhza'a is not far to the east of Khan Younis. It is very close to the 1948 Green Line, the border with Israel. This area has always suffered the brunt of the Israeli attacks, even in quiet times. Frequently, since 2000, the Israeli army has invaded Ikhza'a and the surrounding area; demolishing houses and destroying vast tracts of agricultural land. The best carnations were produced here (and at Beit Lahia in the north of the Gaza Strip). Farmers always boasted about the quality of their flowers. The local economy depended heavily on their cultivation. The farmers had no choice but to sell the flowers to the Israeli Agrexco company which had a monopoly on the production of flowers in the Gaza Strip (the company has now gone into liquidation). The same story of exploitation all over Palestine was repeated here in Ikhza'a: Agrexco would only buy the carnations from the farmers for a very low price, 15 agoras per carnation (there are 100 agoras to one Israeli shekel). However, for the farmers this was the only way to survive as they were not allowed to export their flowers anywhere else. Palestinian flowers always ended up in European markets, sold for very profitable prices.

'When the Apache helicopter hovered over our house on the afternoon of 13 January 2009 there was no reason to be worried,' Ghada Qdaih recounted. 'The Israeli army had declared a ceasefire from 2 p.m. till 4 p.m. My husband Jamil went out to see some of his relatives and make sure that they were safe after the attacks in the morning.

'We were having lunch at approximately 1.30 p.m. and we heard someone shouting outside. My 15-year-old son Muhammad went out to check. It was one of our relatives asking for help to carry his family's belongings as he had decided to leave the area for a safer one. Muhammad helped him. I asked him to stay there as it was safer. He came back half an hour later: he said there was no place like home. I wished he had stayed away. At about 3.15 he asked me if he could go to the shop across the road to buy chocolate for himself and his brother and sisters. His last words were, "Mum, I have a headache, I want to buy chocolate and come back to sleep." He is now asleep forever,' Ghada sighed.

'Minutes later I heard a massive explosion. The Apache helicopters had shelled civilians outside the grocery shop. I went outside and started screaming at the horrifying sight of human bits scattered all over the street. Najy Qdaih, the shop owner survived. Five other civilians were killed in the same attack.[25]

'Muhammad was lying on the ground outside the shop in pain from an injury to the back of his head. Eventually, he was transferred to Nasser Hospital in Khan Younis. He was tall; his legs were too long for the stretcher. I was told by people who witnessed his killing that he was eating a bar of chocolate when he was hit by the rocket.

'The doctors could not save his life due to internal bleeding. He was pronounced dead at 9.30 in the evening. The doctors told us later his condition was moderate in severity. The failure of the ambulance to reach him on time because of the arbitrary shelling by the Israeli army was detrimental to him and his condition worsened. They arrived at the scene after approximately half an hour. To me, he looked like an angel after he died, despite the fact his head was shattered at the back.'

'I went to the Al To'aimat area during the truce to check on some relatives,' Jamil said. 'A rocket landed 10 metres away from me then the shelling intensified. I ran and hid in a nearby house for an hour. When the shelling stopped for a while, I returned home and

---

[25] Yassir Qdaih, Ghassan Abu Rjaila, Mamdouh Abu Rook, Alaa Abu Reidah and Suleiman Abu Qdaih.

went in through the back door. I was told Muhammad had been killed. When I opened the front door I saw the severed head of one of the victims, Alaa'a Abu Reida. Other parts of the bodies were thrown everywhere. The body of my brother Yassir Qdaih was split in half.

'In my confusion I made a terrible mistake: I took my three daughters out of the house in the direction of the massacre. They were shocked by the scene; my 4-year-old daughter Nisreen stepped on a piece of shrapnel and was injured. Nisreen is still very much shaken: she receives psychological treatment here at one of the local clinics. She remembers Muhammad constantly; he used to play with her all the time. She remembers how he used to throw her in the air and then catch her. "Where is Muhammad?" Nisreen always asks. We tell her he is in heaven. She then replies, "His friends are here, why does not he come down?"'

'My eldest daughter Narmin wrote a powerful letter mourning the death of her brother,' Ghada said. 'If I give birth to one hundred kids, I will not have someone like Muhammad.

'We have one boy and three girls; Muhammad was the eldest. His life was very sweet; he was a member of a local football team. We own a piece of land in the middle of a residential area nearby. One day Muhammad took pieces of timber, tools and built a goal post on the land. He used to play there with his friends. Some of the neighbours were annoyed because of the noise. One of them kept telling him off. She came to me after he was killed; she told me how much she regretted that. She cried a lot and kept saying Muhammad never answered back.

'He was a very intelligent pupil. He scored 98 per cent in his last year at school. At the end of every school term, I threw away the school papers of my other children. I never threw away any of Muhammad's stuff. Yesterday, I hugged his pencils and books and cried. He was lovely. At school there is a photo of him with his schoolmates. I asked the headteacher to give it to me; she said, "Ghada, Muhammad was popular – all his classmates want to see this photo all the time." I took a photo of the photo.'

'Muhammad was a member of the children's parliament in our area,' Jamil recounted. 'He won a prize for his work at the parliament but was killed before receiving it. His colleagues came to the house to present me with the prize: it was a very emotional moment. We felt so proud. I told my wife, "Even after his death Muhammad continues to earn a lot of respect through his manners and hard work." Ghada cried a lot that day out of a mixture of pride and sorrow.

'Muhammad had a cat which he loved greatly. He asked me once if he could take a shower with her. I did not mind. He entered the shower then started screaming: the shampoo got in the cat's eyes and she clung to him. We still remember this and laugh a lot.'

Muhammad's brother Wael (16) added, 'I have mixed feelings: a strong desire for revenge and the other for my family and how much they need me – how devastated they would be if anything happened to me.'

'When Wael plays football now he kicks the ball so aggressively,' Jamil said. 'I am very worried about him; he is an extremely angry young man. Once I took the ball off him. I told him I would give it back to him only if he plays as he used to: he promised to try his best. He is a good boy; I hope we will not lose him for no reason.'

'I was putting a lot of hope in Muhammad,' Ghada said. 'His father's situation is really difficult. We thought, "We will be patient and our kids will compensate us for the hardship we suffer." We lost Muhammad, who was the brightest among his brothers and sisters. I tried my best to create an atmosphere in which he would be able to study quietly. I used to ask his brothers and sisters to leave the room. I recognized his potential and I wanted him to fulfil it.'

'To be frank, and no offence to you, I am fed up of people coming to hear our story and nothing happening,' Jamil said. We were very upset, all the organizations wanted to put their flags on his body but I refused and insisted he be buried wrapped in our flag, the flag of Palestine. We are not affiliated to any political organizations. We regard ourselves as Palestinians first and foremost. When we buried him we could not bury him in the cemetery: it was dangerous to do so at the time because of the Israeli army's random shelling. We had to bury him near our house. He was a quiet, gentle and devout young man. What had Muhammad done to them to deserve to be killed in this vicious way? He was a child, not a resistance fighter. Was he going to hurt the Israelis with a chocolate bar? Is this fair? They want to finish us off. These criminals who did this must be brought to justice.'

19

Don't worry Hamada, things are going to get better

After visiting the Qdaih family I was due to meet the family of another victim in the same area. They lived just half a kilometre eastwards, very close to the border. I was warned by the Qdaih family to be careful. They thought I did not show enough concern about their warning. Ghada put her hand on my shoulder and gently emphasized that they were exceptionally serious. People there are always scared to move anywhere within the area. The Israeli army randomly fires at their houses without reason or warning.

'We were asleep on 11 January 2009,' Aziza Abu Rouk remembered. 'Shortly after midnight, the Israeli army started to shell the houses. I woke my children up. I left my house with my children, fleeing the arbitrary shelling. We headed to relatives' houses. The sky was full of red; we were told later it was from the phosphorus bombs. I heard my sisters-in-law screaming; there were fires everywhere. Within five minutes of leaving, we were hit by shrapnel that slightly injured my disabled daughter, Safiya.

'My son Abdullah went to help putting out fires. He was very brave; he did not care about the fire. He wanted to help people.

'After extinguishing the fires everyone ran for cover. The drone launched a rocket on people who were running away,' Aziza continued. 'Phosphorus bombs were also exploding nearby. Abdullah was hit: his leg was blown off. The Israeli army declared the area a military zone. The ambulances could not get to him because of random and intense shelling from the air and from tanks by the Israeli army. After approximately one hour, the ambulances arrived. He was taken to the hospital in Khan Younis then transferred to a hospital in Egypt. He suffered damage to the liver, kidneys and intestines. Before he left for Egypt he was still conscious, he said to me, "Mum, I'm thirsty, I'm hungry." Those were his last words to me. He died in Egypt on the morning of 23 January 2009. There were various injuries amongst the people. Most people who were injured were women and children running for cover. There were no resistance members in our area at that time.

'Abdullah was in the second year at secondary school. He was an average student but always tried his best to improve. I have three daughters and a son left. Our house is still partially damaged since the war. We cannot afford the cost of rebuilding. He was a very good son: in my eyes, the kindest on earth. He was always there for me when I needed him. They took a very promising young man away from me.

'The whole family is still in shock. My daughter Shaima, who is 14 years old, is still having nightmares. I lost part of my eyesight as a result.

'They definitely knew he was a civilian; they must have watched the whole event, seen him extinguishing the fires. They lie to the world; they say they want peace. He never hurt any Israeli. It is not about attacking resistance fighters: it is about wanting to kill the Palestinian, to finish us off. Three of Abdullah's classmates, Nabil To'aimah, Osama Abu Rjaila and Mamdouh Qdaih, were also killed during the war near here. Somehow the Israelis are justifying it and, in a way, getting away with murder. How can this be allowed to happen?

'Abdullah used to sing sad songs all the time. His father Muhammad told me he had discovered in one of his notebooks Abdullah had written how many days he lived so far. He hated bad times. Once, one of the Americans working for a Palestinian non-governmental organization, who lived in our area, was burgled. Abdullah was outraged: he wrote a piece in his notebook ridiculing those who did that. His style was very sarcastic, very funny.

Muhammad read it to me. In the piece Abdullah described these criminals sarcastically as those who do such a terrible thing and yet regard themselves as truly patriotic Palestinians. "Salute the heroes who carried out this heroic operation; who stormed a very fortified Zionist military outpost and fought the invaders," he wrote.

'He had the potential to be a novelist,' Muhammad said. 'He always commented humorously in his writings on social issues. He was a good reader. All our dreams were centered on him. One press of a button from an Israeli soldier destroyed our family. He was my greatest hope. Even when I want to do the simplest of DIY jobs around the house, I remember him. I am getting older; I was hoping that he would be the pillar to support his brothers and sisters.

'He always planted mint and greens, peppers, aubergines. He was good at gardening. He helped the family from a very early age; he frequently took the vegetables to the local market to sell to support us.

'I know a little bit about Judaism: to follow their religion correctly they should stop killing the innocent,' Muhammad continued. 'We wanted peace but they do not care. We offered compromises but they would not listen. How can they claim to want peace when they are killing us all the time? They are wrong if they think that they can finish us off, they won't. The tide will turn, if they continue to be this aggressive. We do not want compensation: even if we got 100 million dollars, it would not compensate us for our beloved Abdullah. We ask for understanding and support: we hope his blood has not been spilled in vain, and that his killers will be brought to justice.'

'The night of his killing he asked me to prepare supper for him,' Aziza said, 'but then he decided not to eat. I'm very sad that he died thirsty and hungry. I see him in my dreams. His father has seen him at least twenty times. He always comes to his brother, Hamada, in his dreams; he always tells him, "Do not worry, brother, things are going to be better." We all suffer from depression.'

Abdullah's eldest sister was crying throughout my talk with her parents. She said to me, 'I wish I would die to get rid of this pain.'

Her father hugged her and told her, 'Remember what Abdullah said to Hamada in his dreams: things are going to get better.'

Shaima, the youngest sister, remembered that once Abdullah insulted someone. 'He could not sleep that night. The following day, early in the morning, he went to apologize. That is how kind and harmless he was.'

'We had one of his photos enlarged. Every day we look at it. I talk to the photo for hours as if he was still alive,' Aziza said, love evident in her eyes.

'I am unemployed at present. I have invested in a number of beehives here at the side of my house; it just helps us get by,' Muhammad said. 'Abdullah was very short; I used to joke with him: I will give you an injection so that you will get taller. He would look at me and laugh. We long for the day when we will be together again. In my dreams I had six snakes about to attack me. When I wanted to kill them he came to me saying, "Do not worry, Dad, I will protect you." He is even helping me when he is dead.'

'I hope whoever killed my son will suffer the same – them and their families. They broke my heart into pieces. They do not care about our suffering,' Aziza said.

Muhammad interrupted, 'I disagree; we only want the killers to suffer, not their families.'

Conclusion

The message from all the families I met during the preparation of this book was crystal clear: 'We will not start to cope with the horrors we suffered until those responsible for these crimes are brought to justice: this will be our only true compensation. How come they have escaped justice all this time? This is double standards. The civilians who supported such attacks are indirectly guilty.' As for the American and European governments which supply Israel with weapons, there was a consensus among the families of the victims that they were directly responsible for what happened.

Another important point many of them emphasized: Israel claimed the war was on Hamas. What we and others like us suffered proved that it was not: it was on us civilians.

According to their testimonies (which were obtained under oath) none of their loved ones killed by the Israeli army during Operation Cast Lead belonged to paramilitary organizations. All the dead were unarmed civilians: there were no armed resistance fighters at the scene at the time of the killings.

There was a consensus among them: they don't want revenge; justice is more important than revenge. They also expressed dissatisfaction with the position of the Arab countries – they just stopped at condemnation but took no concrete steps to stop the slaughter. No serious actions have been taken by any of these governments or the UN to bring justice to us.

They are grateful that some good people in the West are trying to bring those responsible to justice. However, we have very little faith the Western governments will seriously work on this issue. It always seems Israel is above international law

The horrific trauma all the families went through is still affecting them nearly four years after the war has ended. All of the mothers I met are still shaken by what they experienced. To them the lost loved ones were so special that it is extremely difficult to cope. Events like the school graduation of their children or the feasts of Eid bring a mixture of feelings; happiness for the living but a more prominent feeling of sorrow for the lost loved ones.

The emotional vacuum left by the deaths is still being felt by all the families. Some of them lost practical support as well: they relied on their sons to support the family. Some of the victims were the eldest children in their families; the parents lived in hope that, according to the Palestinian culture, they would support their younger brothers and sisters.

The quote coincidently repeated by many of the families of the victims still rings in my ears: 'One press of a button from an Israeli soldier destroyed our family.'

The Statute of the International Criminal Court defines war crimes as, 'serious violations of the laws and customs applicable in international armed conflict' (ICC Statute, Article 8 (cited in Vol. II, Ch. 44, § 3)).[26]

The majority of war crimes involve death, injury, destruction or unlawful taking of property. However, not all acts necessarily have to result in actual damage to persons or objects in order to amount to war crimes. It was decided, for example, that it was enough to launch an attack on civilians or civilian objects, even if something unexpectedly prevented the attack from causing death or serious injury. This could be the case of an attack launched against the civilian population or individual civilians, even though, owing to the failure of the weapon system, the intended target was not hit.

---

[26] Please note the footnotes and references for this Conclusion are © 2012 International Committee of the Red Cross.

[27] See Knut Dörmann, *Elements of War Crimes under the Rome Statute of the International Criminal Court: Sources and Commentary* (Cambridge: Cambridge University Press, 2003) pp. 130 and 233.

Actual injury is not required for the act to amount to a war crime.[27]

To amount to a war crime to be included in the Statute, the conduct had to amount to a violation of a customary rule of international law. An example of violations of customary international law being used as a basis for war criminality is the resolution adopted by consensus in the UN Commission on Human Rights declaring that Israel's 'continuous grave breaches' of the Fourth Geneva Convention and Additional Protocol I were war crimes.[28]

This list of grave breaches was included in the Geneva Conventions largely on the basis of crimes pursued after the Second World War by the International Military Tribunals at Nuremberg and at Tokyo and by national courts. The list is repeated in the Statutes of the International Criminal Tribunal for the former Yugoslavia and of the International Criminal Court (ICTY Statute, Article 2; ICC Statute, Article 8(2)(a)).

The war crime 'making medical or religious personnel, medical units or medical transports the object of attack' covers aspects of the war crime contained in the Statute of the International Criminal Court (ICC Statute, Article 8(2)(b)(ix) and (xxiv)). Many of the incidents during the attack on the Gaza Strip fall under this rule: the attack on the ambulance which was carrying Yassir Shbair (see ch. 5, p. 25); the numerous incidents where ambulances and medical staff were prevented from reaching the injured are clear examples; and the attack on Al Quds hospital in Gaza City (see Introduction, p. xx).

'Making the civilian population or individual civilians, not taking a direct part in hostilities, the object of attack.' There are numerous examples of national legislation which make it a criminal offence to direct attacks against civilians, including the legislation of States not, or not at the time, party to Additional Protocol I.[29] The attack on the Deeb family (see ch. 1, p. 5), on the UN Al Fakhora

---

28 UN Commission on Human Rights, Res. 1982/1 (ibid. § 98).

29 See legislation (cited in Vol. II, Ch. 1, §§ 217–269), in particular the legislation of Azerbaijan (ibid., §§ 221–222), Indonesia (ibid., § 243) and Italy (ibid., § 245).

school in Jabalia and the killing of the Abed Rabu sisters and Rawhia Al Najar (see Introduction, p. xix) when they were waving a white flag is clearly relevant to the above rule.

'Launching an attack in the knowledge that such attack will cause incidental loss of civilian life, injury to civilians or damage to civilian objects which would be clearly excessive in relation to the concrete and direct military advantage anticipated.' Numerous States have adopted legislation making it an offence to carry out an attack which violates the principle of proportionality.[30] The attack on the Al Samouny compound (see ch. 15, p. 93) is an example of this rule.

It is an offence to attack non-defended localities. In addition, such attacks would arguably constitute the war crime of 'making civilian objects, that is, objects that are not military objectives, the object of attack' or 'making the civilian population or individual civilians, not taking a direct part in hostilities, the object of attack' contained in the Statute (Article 8(2)(b)(i) and (ii)). The attack on hundreds of civilian institutes during the war is the relevant example here.

Making buildings dedicated to religion, education, art, science or charitable purposes or historic monuments the object of attack, provided they are not military objectives, is a clear violation of customary international law. It is also a war crime in the Statute of the International Criminal Court.[31] The attacks on 23 mosques and the

---

[30] See, e.g., the legislation of Armenia (cited in Vol. II, Ch. 4, § 50), Australia (*ibid.*, §§ 51–52), Belarus (*ibid.*, § 53), Belgium (*ibid.*, § 54), Canada (*ibid.*, §§ 57–58), Colombia (*ibid.*, § 59), Congo (*ibid.*, § 60), Cook Islands (*ibid.*, § 61), Cyprus (*ibid.*, § 62), Georgia (*ibid.*, § 64), Germany (*ibid.*, § 65), Ireland (*ibid.*, § 66), Mali (*ibid.*, § 68), Netherlands (*ibid.*, § 69), New Zealand (*ibid.*, §§ 70–71), Niger (*ibid.*, § 73), Norway (*ibid.*, § 74), Spain (*ibid.*, § 75), Sweden (*ibid.*, § 76), United Kingdom (*ibid.*, §§ 78–79) and Zimbabwe (*ibid.*, § 80); see also the draft legislation of Argentina (*ibid.*, § 49), Burundi (*ibid.*, § 56), El Salvador (*ibid.*, § 63), Lebanon (*ibid.*, § 67), Nicaragua (*ibid.*, § 72) and Trinidad and Tobago (*ibid.*, § 77).

[31] Additional Protocol I, Article 85(3) and (4); ICC Statute, Article 8(2)(b).

Islamic university during the war are relevant here.

According to the Statute of the International Criminal Court 'launching an attack in the knowledge that such attack will cause widespread, long-term and severe damage to the natural environment which would be clearly excessive in relation to the concrete and direct military advantage anticipated.' In addition, a deliberate attack on the environment, not required by military necessity, would also amount to a war crime because it would in effect be an attack on a civilian object (see Rule 7). The attack by the Israeli air force which destroyed Al Nimir Water Wells Complex in Jabalia (see Introduction, p. xxi). Also the bombing of the sewage treatment tanks in Gaza City (see Introduction, p. xxi) and the destruction of agricultural land during the ground invasion are relevant to this rule.

Using prohibited weapons that are of a nature to cause superfluous injury or unnecessary suffering or which are inherently indiscriminate must also be subject to a 'comprehensive prohibition' and listed in an annex to the Statute.[32] The use of white phosphorus during attacks on residential areas and the use of the internationally prohibited flechette tank shells by the Israeli army (see Introduction, p. xvi) fall under the above mentioned rule.

Collective punishments are listed as a war crime in the legislation of numerous States.[33] The siege of Gaza; travel restrictions on 1.5 million people for long periods; cutting electricity and water supplies; and the frequent destruction of agricultural land in the West Bank and the Gaza Strip are clear examples of collective punishment.

There are no wars without perpetrators. Those who planned,

---

[32] ICC Statute, Article 8(2)(b)(xx) (cited in Vol. II, Ch. 20, § 405).

[33] See, e.g., the legislation of Argentina (cited in Vol. II, Ch. 32, § 3776), Australia (*ibid.*, § 3777), Bangladesh (*ibid.*, § 3778), Bosnia and Herzegovina (*ibid.*, § 3779), China (*ibid.*, § 3780), Democratic Republic of the Congo (*ibid.*, § 3781), Côte d'Ivoire (*ibid.*, § 3782), Croatia (*ibid.*, § 3783), Ethiopia (*ibid.*, § 3784), Ireland (*ibid.*, § 3785), Italy (*ibid.*, § 3786), Kyrgyzstan (*ibid.*, § 3787), Lithuania (*ibid.*, § 3788), Norway (*ibid.*, § 3789), Romania (*ibid.*, § 3790), Slovenia (*ibid.*, § 3791), Spain (*ibid.*, § 3792) and Yugoslavia (*ibid.*, § 3793).

ordered and executed the assault on Gaza knew full well the likely consequences in civilian lives. They must be brought to justice. If for now that seems a remote possibility we must not assume it cannot be achieved. We owe it to the victims to battle for justice.

Appendix 1:

The Gaza Strip

Palestine Monitor Fact Sheet

The Facts

Total Population:	1,500,202
Population Density:	4117 per sq km
Fertility Rate:	5.19 children/woman
Total Refugees:	1,059,584 (UNRWA)
Refugees as % of Population:	70%
Unemployment:	45.5%
Average Age:	17.2 years – some estimates have put the median age at 15.3.
Life Expectancy:	73.16 years
% dependant on foreign aid:	86%

Area

Area:	total: 360 sq km land: 360 sq km water: 0 sq km
Area – comparative:	slightly more than twice the size of Washington, DC
Land boundaries:	total: 62 km
Border countries:	Egypt 11 km, Israel 51 km

Coastline:	40 km
Climate:	temperate, mild winters, dry and warm to hot summers
Terrain:	flat to rolling, sand- and dune-covered coastal plain
Natural resources:	arable land, natural gas
Land use:	arable land: 28.95% permanent crops: 21.05% other: 50% (2001)
Irrigated land:	120 sq km (1998 est.)
Environment – current issues:	desertification; salination of fresh water; sewage treatment; water-borne disease; soil degradation; depletion and contamination of underground water resources
Population growth rate:	3.77% (2005 est.)
Ethnic groups:	Palestinian Arab

Economy Overview

Labour force – by occupation:	agriculture 14%, industry 19%, services 66% (2004)
Unemployment rate:	50% (includes West Bank) (2003 est.)
Agriculture products:	olives, citrus, vegetables; beef, dairy products
Industries:	generally small family businesses that produce textiles, soap, olive-wood carvings, and mother-of-pearl souvenirs; the Israelis have established some small-scale modern industries in an industrial centre
Economic aid – recipient:	$2 billion (includes West Bank) (2004 est.)
Currency (code):	new Israeli shekel (ILS)

Transportation

Highways	total: NA km paved: NA km unpaved: NA km note: small, poorly developed road network
Ports and harbours:	Gaza
Airports:	Gaza International Airport (GIA), inaugurated on 24 November 1998 as part of agreements stipulated in the September 1995 Oslo II Accord and the 23 October 1998 Wye River Memorandum; GIA has been largely closed since October 2000 by Israeli orders and its runway was destroyed by the Israeli occupation army in December 2001 (2004 est.)

Appendix 2:

Maps

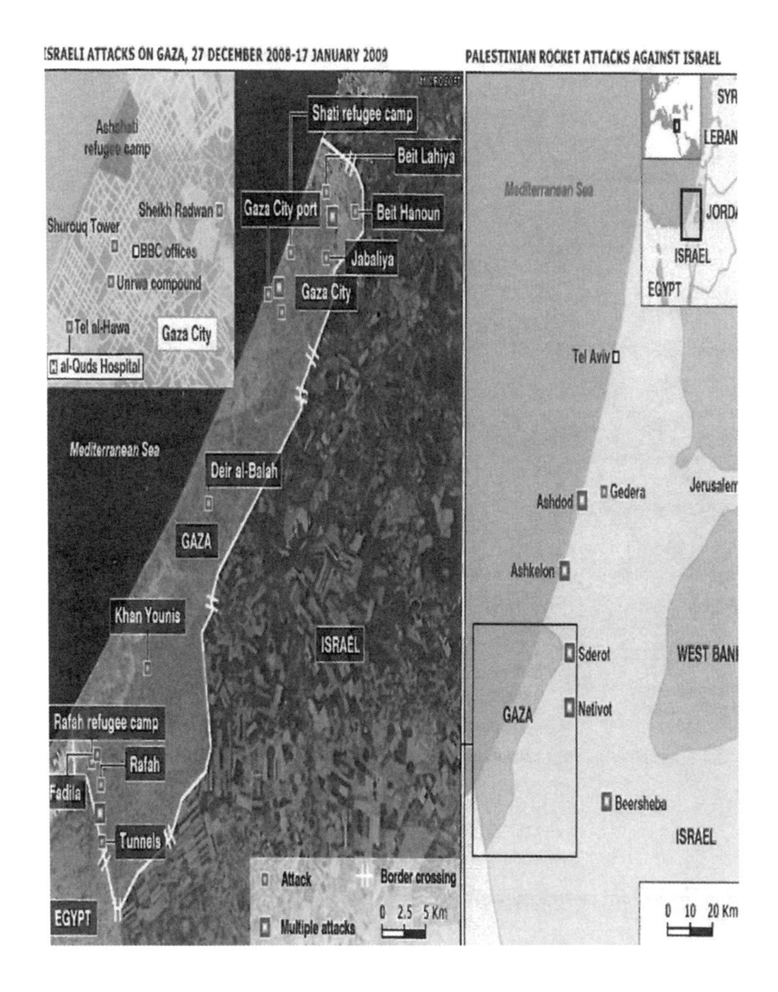

(Previous page) Map of the attacks on Gaza

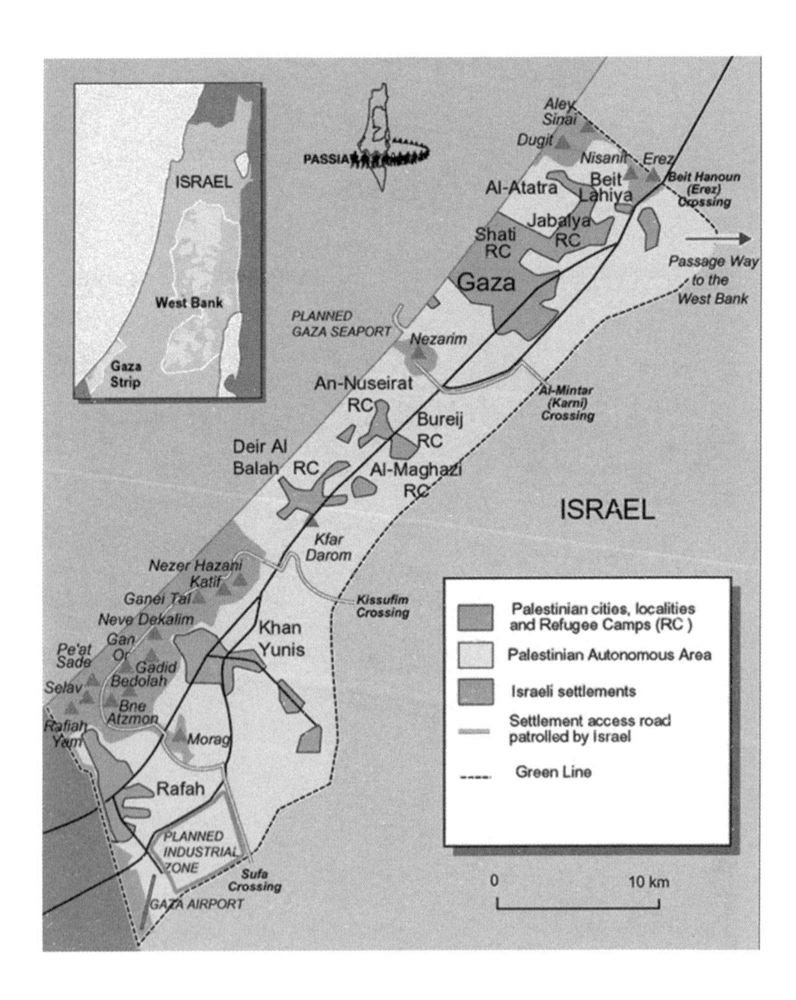

(Above) Israeli Settlements

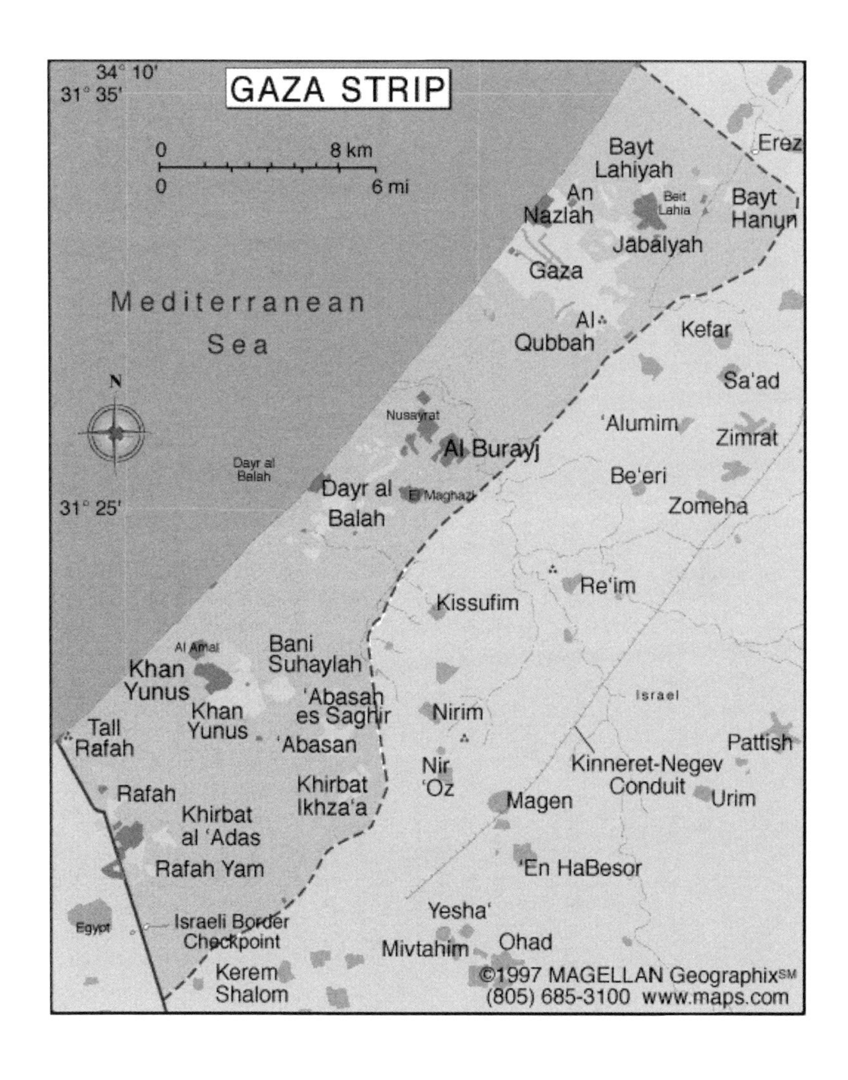
GAZA STRIP
34° 10'
31° 35'
31° 25'
0 8 km
0 6 mi
Mediterranean
Sea
N
Bayt
Lahiyah
Erez
An
Nazlah
Beit
Lahia
Bayt
Hanun
Jabalyah
Gaza
Al
Qubbah
Kefar
Sa'ad
Nusayrat
'Alumim
Zimrat
Al Burayj
Dayr al
Balah
Be'eri
Dayr al
Balah
El Maghazi
Zomeha
Re'im
Kissufim
Al Amal
Bani
Suhaylah
Khan
Yunus
'Abasah
es Saghir
Nirim
Israel
Khan
Yunus
Tall
Rafah
'Abasan
Pattish
Nir
'Oz
Kinneret-Negev
Conduit
Rafah
Khirbat
Ikhza'a
Magen
Urim
Khirbat
al 'Adas
Rafah Yam
'En HaBesor
Yesha'
Egypt
Israeli Border
Checkpoint
Mivtahim
Ohad
Kerem
Shalom
©1997 MAGELLAN Geographix℠
(805) 685-3100 www.maps.com

Appendix 3:

Timeline

Wednesday 21 January

- Israeli troops completed their withdrawal from the Gaza Strip

Tuesday 20 January

- Aid agencies said that some parts of the Gaza Strip worst-hit by the Israeli attacks look as if they have been hit by a sizable earthquake.

- Palestinian medical staff and rescue teams continued to recover bodies from under the rubble. Correspondents in the Gaza Strip confirmed that entire neighbourhoods have been flattened by Israeli tanks and air strikes.

- UN sources stated that as a result of Operation Cast Lead, 400,000 people have no running water. The UN also confirmed that it is still sheltering more than 35,000 Palestinians.

Monday 19 January

- The Palestinian Authority's Central Bureau of Statistics said that more than 1,400 Palestinians died and about 5,400 others were wounded and more than 22,000 houses were either partly or completely destroyed during Israel's three-week offensive.

Sunday 18 January

- Hamas and other Palestinian organizations in the Gaza Strip declared they would stop attacks on Israel for a week. They also demanded Israel remove troops from Gaza.

Saturday 17 January

- Israel announced a unilateral ceasefire in the fighting beginning at 2 a.m. local time on Sunday. Israeli Prime Minister Ehud Olmert said troops would remain in Gaza for now.

- Israel carried out more than 50 air raids on different parts of the Gaza Strip overnight

- In Jabaliya refugee camp, two children, aged five and seven, were killed by Israeli tank fire inside a UN school where hundreds had taken shelter. UN spokesperson, Chris Gunness, demanded an investigation to find out whether a war crime has been committed. Israel rejected the demand.

Friday 16 January

- More than 40 air strikes were carried out on different targets during the night.

- Israeli tanks withdrew from Gaza City in the early hours of the morning.

- Palestinian medical teams and volunteers pulled 23 bodies from the rubble in the Tel Al-Hawa area of Gaza City.

- A teenager was killed in Hebron in clashes between protesters and Israeli forces.

- No injuries were reported following the launching of over 10 rockets from the Gaza Strip into southern Israel.

Thursday 15 January

- Hamas interior minister, Said Siyam, was killed when the Israeli Air Force bombed his brother's house. His son, brother and two other Hamas officials were killed in the attack.

- Israeli tanks and troops moved deep into Gaza City following an intense bombardment in the early hours.

- Hundreds of terrified civilians rushed into the streets to try to flee the fighting.

- The Israeli Air Force carried out more than 15 air raids on Palestinian targets in different parts of the Gaza Strip.

- An Israeli soldier was killed and another was severely wounded in a battle near Jabaliya.

- Large parts of Al Quds hospital, in Tel Al-Hawa area in Gaza City, which is run by the Palestinian Red Crescent Society caught fire when it was hit by Israeli tank shells; the hospital was evacuated as result.

- Israeli artillery shells hit a UN compound; tonnes of aid supplies go up in flames as a result.

- More than 15 rockets were fired from the Gaza Strip into southern Israel severely damaging a house in Sderot and wounding five people in Be'er Sheva .

Wednesday 14 January

- Sixty Palestinian targets were struck overnight as the Israeli air raids continued for a nineteenth day. A cemetery was damaged in one of the air raids.

- The Israeli city of Kiryat Shmona in the north was targeted with three Katyusha rockets from southern Lebanon; no casualties or damage were reported. Associated Press news agency reported that the Israeli army retaliated by firing eight shells into southern Lebanon.

Tuesday 13 January

- The Israeli army continued with land, sea and air bombardment of different parts of the Gaza Strip for an eighteenth day. Sixty targets were hit overnight according to Israeli sources.
- The day witnessed advancement of Israeli troops into the southern and eastern parts of Gaza City.

- An Israeli officer and two soldiers were injured by an explosion in the northern Gaza Strip.

- Israeli bombardment of Palestinian areas was reported during a three-hour ceasefire held to allow Palestinians to seek food, water and other supplies.

- 25 mortars and rockets have been fired into the southern part of Israeli with no casualties reported.

Monday 12 January

- Fierce fighting continued around Gaza City as Israeli forces moved into the most densely populated areas. The Israeli army stated that four soldiers were wounded, one seriously.

- Twelve Israeli air strikes were carried out across the Gaza Strip killing nine Palestinians, five of whom, according to Palestinian officials, were civilians. This is a much lower number of air strikes than recent nights.

- Thirty rockets and mortars were fired at Israel from Gaza during the day with no reports of injuries.

Sunday 11 January

- Al Fadila mosque in Rafah and a Hamas-run school in the southern border region were among 60 targets attacked by the Israeli Air Force.
- At least seven Palestinian civilians were killed and dozens injured when Israeli tank fire hit homes in Beit Lahia and Nussirat

- The Israeli army started to deploy thousands of reservists into the Gaza Strip for the first time since the Israeli offensive started.

- Israeli ground troops moved into heavily populated areas around Gaza City. Heavy clashes erupted in the southern suburb of Sheikh Ajleen. At least 40 Hamas gunmen were killed in this battle according to Israeli and Palestinian sources.

- A woman was killed and dozens of civilians were injured in Israeli shelling of the village of Khouza, east of Khan Younis. Later, Palestinian medics stated that the injured suffered from burns and gas inhalations, symptoms indicating exposure to white phosphorus. Israel rejected the claim.

- Two Palestinian rockets were launched at the city of Beersheba; no causalities reported.

- Israeli sources stated that Hamas operatives tried to shoot down an Israeli fixed wing aircraft with anti-aircraft missiles for the first time since the operation in Gaza begun.

Sunday 10 January

- More than 70 Palestinian targets were attacked on Saturday, following 40 overnight air strikes according to Israeli military sources.

- Eight Palestinian civilians were killed by Israeli tank fire when a tank shell hits a house in Jabaliya town according to Palestinian medical officials.

- More than 30 rockets were fired at the southern Israel including four which landed in the Israeli town of Ashkelon, lightly injuring two people. Other rockets landed in open areas, causing no casualties.

- Israeli ground troops have moved closer to the edge of Gaza City.

Friday 9 January

- The Israeli offensive continued, despite the passing of a UN Security Council resolution calling for an immediate and durable ceasefire. Israel dismissed the Security Council resolution as 'impractical'. Israel said that it launched 50 strikes overnight.

- At least six Palestinians are reported killed in Beit Lahia after their house was struck by Israeli fire.

- Israel denied that about 30 Palestinians from Al Samouny family were killed earlier this week when Israeli forces shelled a house into which they had earlier moved about 100 Palestinian civilians, many of them children.

- At least 30 rockets were fired from Gaza at southern Israel hitting the towns of Ashkelon, Ashdod and Beersheba. No casualties were reported.

Gaza City under attack
(Ashraf Amra)

A cemetery bombed by the Israeli army
(Ashraf Amra)

Families sheltering in one of the UN Schools before it was bombed (Ewa Jasiewicz)

White phosphorus burning inside a UN School where civilians were sheltering under attack (Ewa Jasiewicz)

A nursery within Al Quds hospital compound in Gaza City
(Ewa Jasiewicz)

An attack on a government civilian building
(Sharif Sarhan)

One of many mosques destroyed by the Israeli Air Force (Ewa Jasiewicz)

One of the many Palestinian Red Crescent Ambulances that were bombed (Ashraf Amra)

Civilians fleeing the Israeli army advance (Ashraf Amra)

UN civilian supplies depot in Gaza bombed by the Israelis (Ashraf Amra)

A father rushing his daughter to hospital (Ashraf Amra)

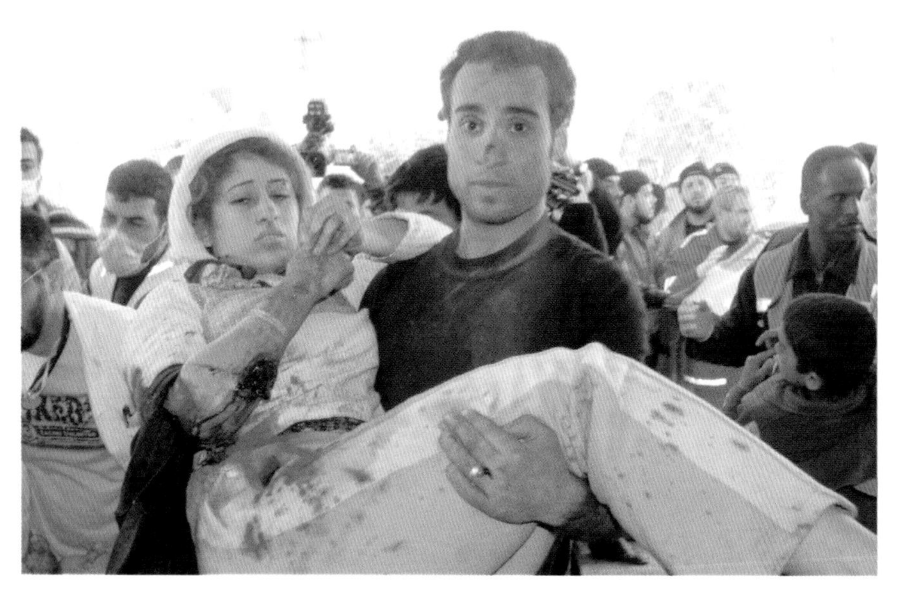

Injured civilians being taken to Al Shifa hospital
(Ashraf Amra)

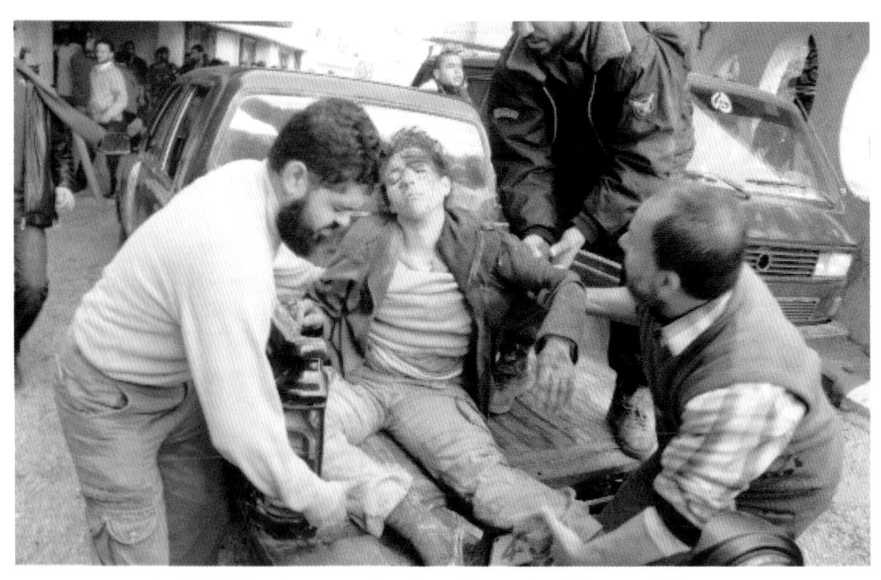

A child being rushed to hospital in a pick-up
(Ashraf Amra)

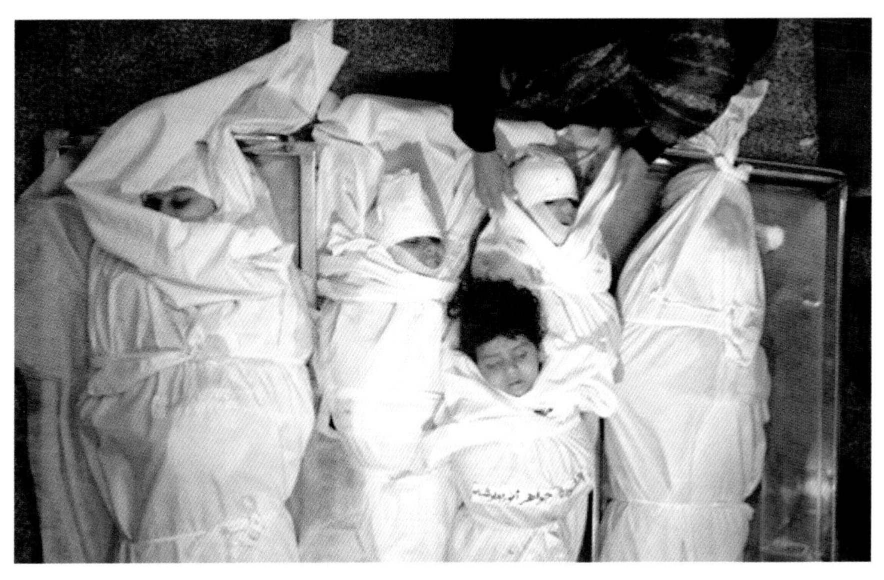

The five Baloosha sisters who were killed while sleeping

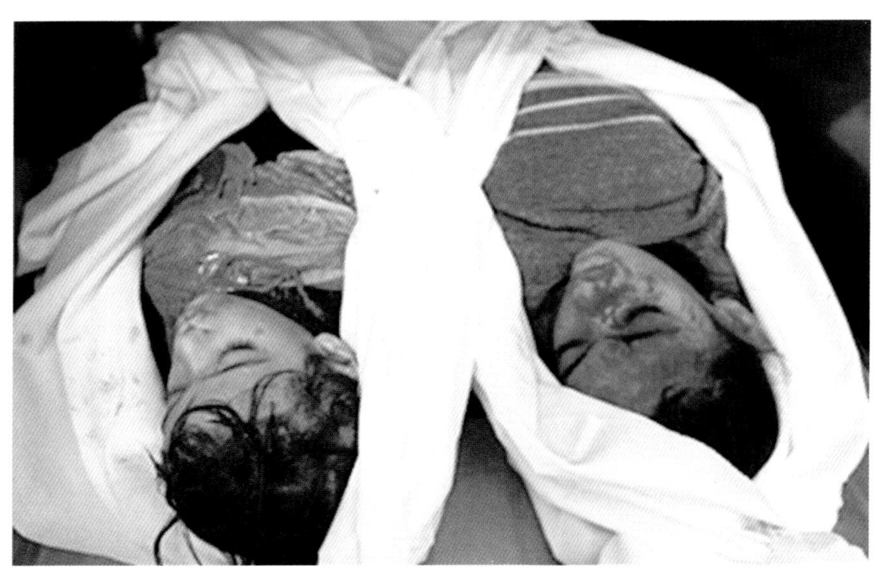

Lama Hamdan (9) and her sister Haya (4)

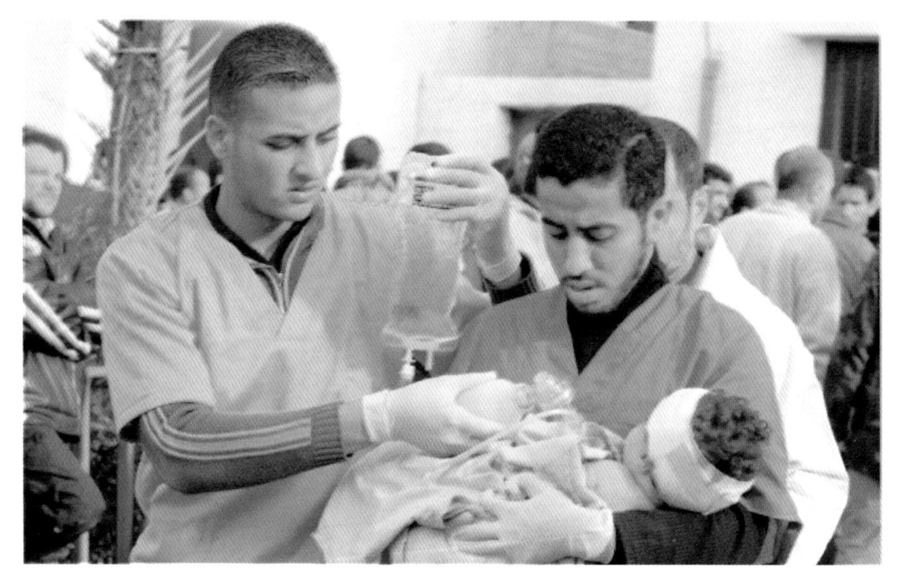

An injured baby being rushed to hospital (Sharif Sarhan)

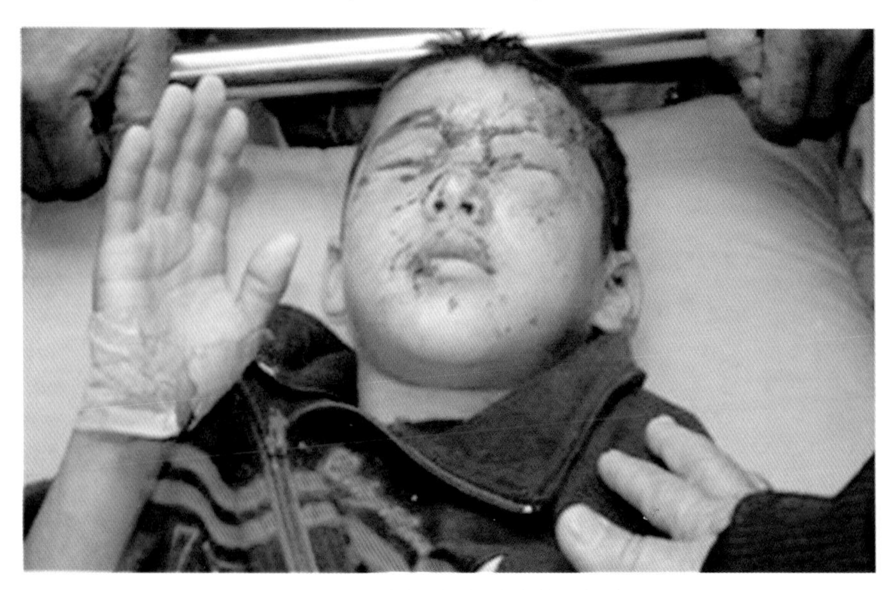

Louai Sobboh (11) blinded by the attacks

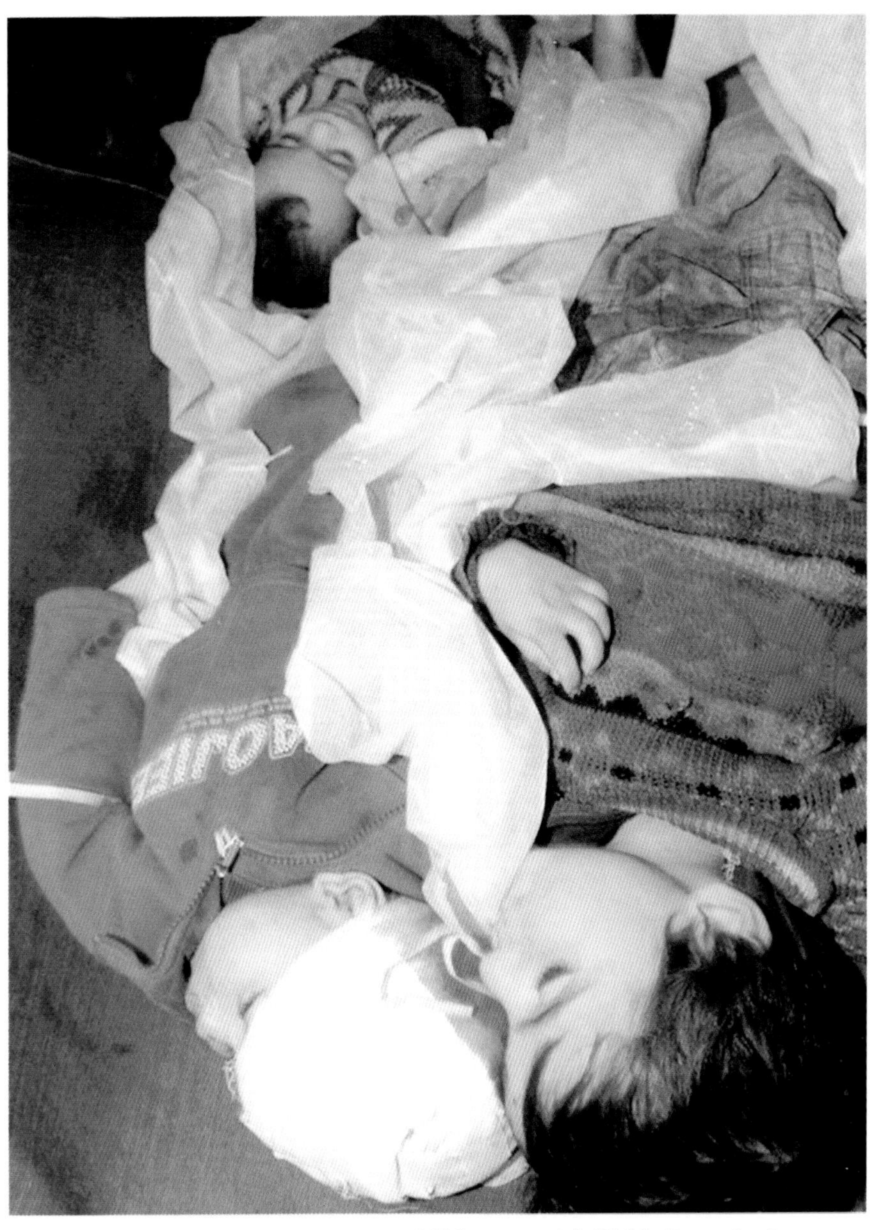

Bodies of three young children at Al Shifa hospital
(Sharif Sarhan)

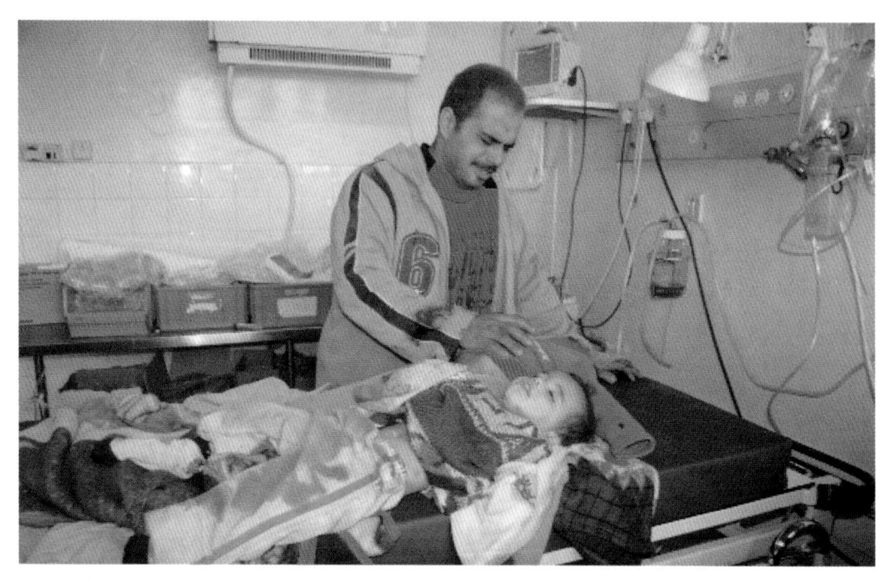

A father with the bodies of his children at Al Shifa hospital
(Ashraf Amra)

A child during one of the frequent power cuts
(Sharif Sarhan)

Civilians trying to salvage some belongings from the rubbish
(Ashraf Amra)

Civilians queuing for food supplies during the war
(Sharif Sarhan)

A child trying to get warm while others play on the rubble
(Asraf Amra)

Israeli Zionists enjoying the destruction of Gaza

Jews against the massacres

Playing outside tents provided by charities
(Ewa Jasiewicz)

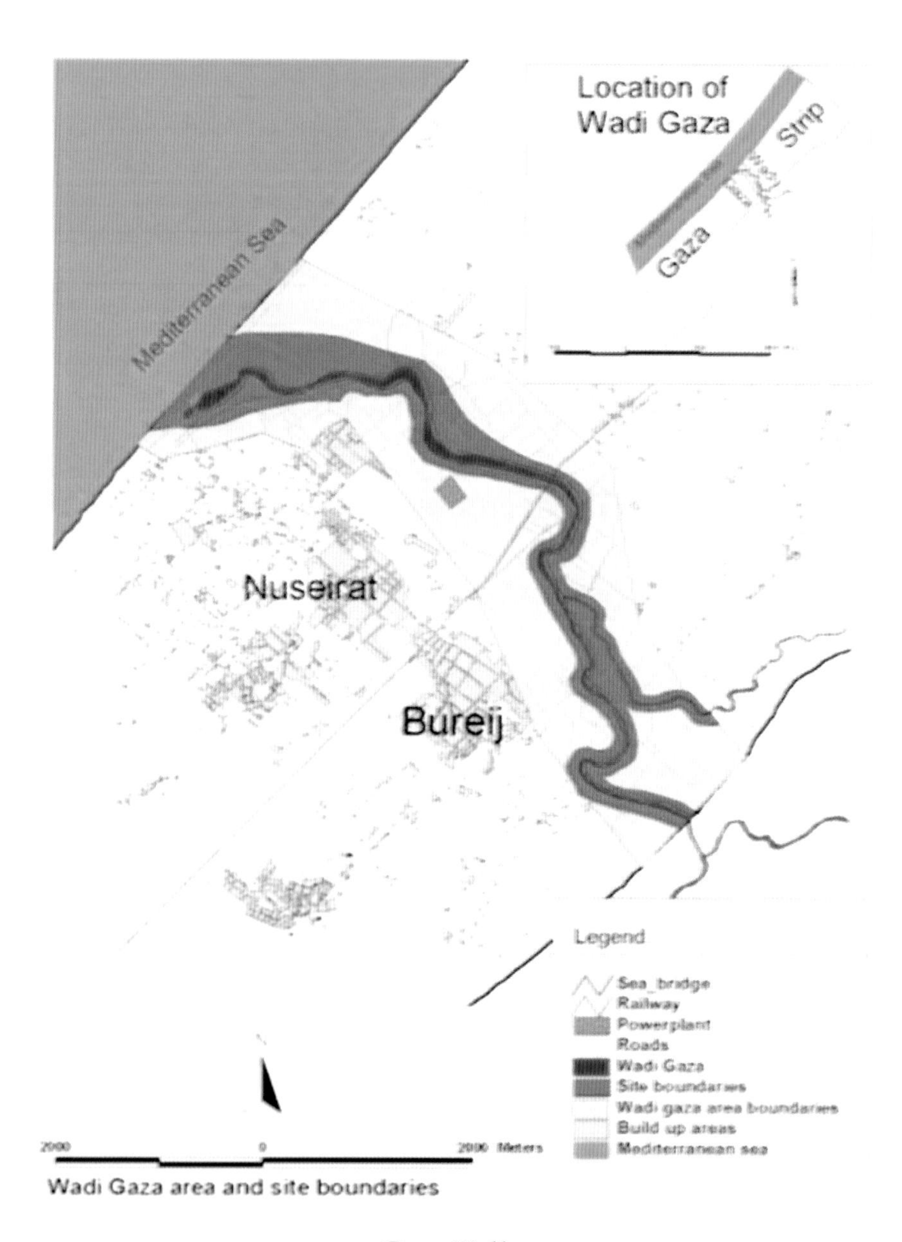

Gaza Valley
(*Wadi Gaza*)

- The UN said its aid workers would resume movement, having received assurances from Israel that they were not being targeted. Operations were suspended after one of the UN drivers was killed.

Thursday 8 January

- 60 Israeli air strikes were launched overnight. Ten people, including civilians, are killed and 22 injured, Palestinian medics said.

- The UN suspended all relief activities in Gaza until it had received guarantees of the safety of its staff from Israel. This was following an Israeli attack on a UN aid convoy which killed at least one driver near Eritz in spite of the UN co-ordinating its movements with the Israeli army.

- The house of a senior Hamas military commander Mohammed al-Senwar, in Khan Younis, was destroyed in an Israeli air strike. Palestinian sources say a mosque was also hit.

- Israel announced the deaths of three soldiers bringing the total number of soldiers killed to eight.

- Three Katyusha rockets from Lebanon territory were fired at the northern Israeli city of Nahariya. Two civilians were injured.

- Rockets fired from Gaza to Southern Israel hit residential area in Ashkelon causing no causalities.

Wednesday 7 January

- Forty air raids were launched by the Israeli Air Force. At least 20 Palestinians were killed in the Gaza Strip.

- Israel initiated a three-hour daily 'humanitarian' truce.
- At least 15 rockets hit southern Israel, causing no casualties.

Tuesday 6 January

- Israel's ground assault entered its fourth day. Heavy fighting was reported between Israeli troops and Palestinian fighters in the north of Gaza city.
- Palestinian medics in Gaza and news agencies worldwide reported, that 43 people were killed including children and 55 injured when Israeli artillery shells landed outside a United Nations-run al-Fakhura school in the Jabaliya refugee camp . UN officials said the school was being used as a refuge for hundreds of people.
- An Israeli air strike on a four-story building in Gaza City the night before killed 12 members of the extended Daya family including seven children aged 1 to 12 years old, three women and two men.
- At least 30 rockets were fired into Israel from the Gaza Strip. Gedera, 30 kilometres south of Tel Aviv, was hit for the first time by a Grad rocket lightly injuring a 3-month old girl.
- Twenty people were killed in a number of Israeli attacks. Medical workers reported that an attack on Deir al-Balah and the Bureij refugee camp killed ten Palestinians, including a father and his three children.
- An Israeli soldier was killed and four wounded in an ambush in northern Gaza City.
- The Israeli Air Force carried out an air raid on Rafah and the main crossing point between the Gaza Strip and Egypt.

- The death toll of the day was at least 70 Palestinians and five Israeli soldiers.

Monday 5 January

- An Israeli air strike hit an ambulance, killing three paramedics.

- Media reported for the first time that Israel was using the controversial substance white phosphorus. According to Ha'aretz and the UN humanitarian chief, Israel had also used cluster bombs.

- A total of 30 Palestinian civilians were known to have been killed on 5 January.

- An official from the Danish charitable organization DanChurchAid reported that three mobile clinics set up to help hospitals in Gaza cope with the wounded were bombarded in Israeli air strikes, despite being clearly marked as humanitarian vehicles.

- Hamas launched over 40 Qassam and Grad rockets at southern Israel striking Ashkelon, Ashdod, Sderot, Kiryat Malakhi, near Ofakim, Netivot and Beersheba.

- The Israeli army claimed that it has destroyed several tunnels and the homes of a number of Hamas officials.

- Heavy clashes were reported east of Gaza City forcing hundreds of people to head further into the city centre to escape the fighting.

Sunday 4 January

- Israeli ground troops entered Beit Lahia and Beit Hanoun in northern Gaza in the early hours. Witnesses report Israeli troops in the Zeitoun area, and that the main north-south road is blocked. Israeli troops took control of the site of the former Jewish settlement of Netzarim.

- At least 17 people were killed and 130 injured when Israeli shells fall near a school and the main market in Gaza City according to Palestinian medical sources.

- A tank shell fired in Beit Lahia killed 12 people, including civilians.

- An Israeli missile hit a house in the Shuja'iyya neighbourhood, killing a mother and her four children.

- An ambulance operating out of Al-Awda hospital in the northern city of Beit Lahia was shelled, seriously injuring four medical staff.

- At least 40 rockets and mortars were fired into Sderot, Netivot. One woman is slightly injured in Sderot.

Saturday 3 January

- Israel launched its first artillery strikes across the border. Hours later Israeli ground troops entered the northern part of the Gaza Strip.

- At least 30 rockets were fired on Ashkelon, Ashdod and Sderot. No casualties were reported. Four Israelis have been killed by rockets fired from Gaza since the beginning of the attacks.

- Thirteen Palestinians, including six children, were killed and dozens wounded when the Israeli Air Force bombed the al-Maqadma mosque in Beit Lahia, in which about 200 people had gathered for evening prayers.

- Israeli war planes destroyed large parts of the town's American school, killing a caretaker.

Friday 2 January

- One of the Israeli strikes in Khan Younis killed five civilians including three children.

- Israel began to bomb the ground near its boundary in an attempt to clear it of landmines, increasing speculation that a ground offensive was imminent.

- An International Red Cross and Red Crescent Movement ambulance was destroyed by an Israeli attack west of Deir al-Balah. The two crew members in the ambulance were injured and hospitalised.

- Thirty rockets were fired at Ashkelon; three people were slightly injured, and several buildings sustained heavy damage.

- The Israeli warplanes destroyed a mosque in Jabaliya. Israeli security officials claimed that it was used to stockpile weapons.

Thursday 1 January

- Israeli air strikes hit Gaza's parliament building (the Legislative Council), and the offices of the education and justice ministries, leaving four dead and 25 wounded.

- Two money changers' offices and a workshop were attacked by Israeli Air Force.
- A one-tonne bomb was dropped by an Israeli jet fighter on the home of Nizar Rayan, a senior Hamas political leader, in the Jabaliya refugee camp, killing him, nine women including his wives and 11 children and wounding another 30.
- Hamas fired more than 50 rockets on southern Israel; one landed in Ashdod and two in Beersheba; no casualties reported.

Wednesday 31 December

- The Office of Hamas Prime Minister Ismail Haniya and other Hamas buildings were attacked.
- Gaza City: the Israeli Air Force continued to strike tunnels near the border with Egypt.
- Hamas attacked Beersheba with rockets for a second day; no casualties reported.
- UNRWA reported that at least 25 per cent of the dead thus far in the conflict had been civilians.
- According to UN humanitarian coordinator Maxwell Gaylard, Gaza's hospitals were facing severe strain dealing with 'their largest ever trauma caseloads under some of the most adverse conditions imaginable'.
- Israel rejected international appeals proposed by the French Foreign Minister Bernard Kouchner to grant a 48-hour ceasefire. Hamas spokesman Ayman Taha told the AFP agency that Hamas is open to any ceasefire proposition that will end the Israeli air strikes and stop the Gaza blockade.

Tuesday 30 December

- The Israeli Air Force completely destroyed the 'whole compound' of ministerial buildings in Gaza City, including the Ministries of Finance and the Interior.

- Two young girls killed in an air strike in Beit Hanoun.
- The Gaza Community Mental Health Programme (GCMHP) premises were destroyed.

- Hamas launched rockets at Beersheba, a city in southern Israel. A Grad missile landed in an empty kindergarten, causing damage but no injuries. An Israeli woman was killed in a rocket attack in Ashdod.

Monday 29 December

- The Israeli Navy attacked the Gaza coast line, using both the Typhoon weapon system and surface-to-surface missiles.
- An Israeli soldier killed and five others wounded in a Palestinian rocket attack at military base near Nahal Oz border crossing.

- One Israeli man was killed and five other people injured in rocket attack in Ashkelon.

- Israeli forces carried out six air strikes just after midnight against the Islamic University of Gaza in the Tel al-Hawa neighbourhood.

- The Palestinian Interior Ministry in Gaza was hit by Israeli missiles at dawn.

Sunday 28 December

- Twenty-five air strikes were carried out on by Israel on Palestinian targets.

- Several civilians including five sisters killed when a mosque was bombed in Jabaliya refugee camp. Three brothers reported killed Yabna refugee camp in Rafah.

- Four members of Islamic Jihad and a child reported killed in Khan Younis.

- Palestinian rockets hit the city of Ashdod, the first attack so far north.

- Al Saraya, a building in Gaza City which contained government offices, security offices and a prison, was des-troyed. Four people died. A fuel lorry traveling in Rafah near the Egyptian border was destroyed, killing six people.
- Israeli jets bombed tunnels running between Egypt and Gaza and claimed successful destruction of 40 of them.

- Gaza City port and intelligence building were attacked by Israeli naval vessels.

- The main road of Salahuddin which leads to the towns of Beit Hanoun, Beit Lahia and Jabalia in northern Gaza Strip was bombed.

Saturday 27 December

- Sixty Israeli F16 fighter jets and AH-64 Apache attack helicopters launched a wave of air and missile attacks on targets in Gaza City, Rafah, and Khan Younis. Reportedly, 225 to 292 people were killed. Most are policemen within the Hamas militant movement; police chief Tawfik Jaber is among the dead. Women and children also died, according to officials in Gaza.

- More than 100 tonnes of bombs were dropped on the Gaza Strip.
- Netivot: One man killed, several injured in Palestinian rocket attack on southern Israel.
- Saturday, the 27 December produced the highest one-day death toll in 60 years of conflict.

Appendix 4: The Accused

The accused (the Israeli political and military leaders in charge during the attacks):

1. Ehud Olmert, in his person and capacity as Prime Minister, member of the Israeli Inner Security Council.

2. Ehud Barak, in his person and capacity as Israeli Defence Minister, member of the Israeli Inner Security Council.

3. Tzipi Livni, in her person and capacity as Foreign Minister of Israel, member of the Israeli Inner Security Council.

4. Gabi Ashkanazi, in his person and capacity as Chief of Staff, the Israeli Defence forces.

5. Brigadier General Yu'af Galnet, in his person and capa-city as Commander of Southern Region.

6. Brigadier General Ayal Abzenberg, in his person and capacity as Commander of the Southern Sector in the Israeli Army.

7. Brigadier General Edo Nahoushen, in his person and capacity as Commander of the Israeli Air Force.

8. Brigadier General Ajay Yehzekily, in his person and capacity as Commander of the Israeli Armoured Corps.

9. Brigadier General Ibli Marom, in his person and capacity as of the Navy.

10. Brigadier General Moshe Shelly Cohen, in his person and capacity as Commander of the Engineers Corps of the Infantry.

11. Colonel Yegal Slovik, in his person and capacity as Commander of 401 armour brigade of the Armour Corps.

12. Colonel Michael Ben Baroch, Commander of Army Intelligence Corps.

13. Ma'er Dagan, Head of Mossad.

14. Yuval Diskin, Head of Shabak.

NOTES

NOTES

NOTES

NOTES

NOTES

NOTES

NOTES

NOTES

NOTES

NOTES

NOTES

NOTES